WITH

TO THE CROSS

A Lenten Guide on the Sunday Mass Readings:
Year A

A Catholic Guide for Small Groups

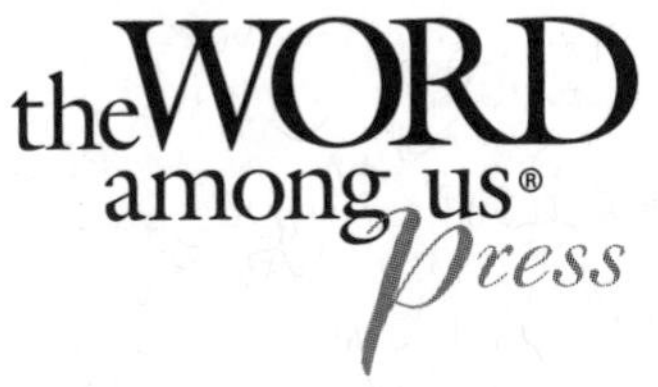

Copyright © 2017 by The Evangelical Catholic
All rights reserved.

Published by The Word Among Us Press
7115 Guilford Drive, Suite 100
Frederick, Maryland 21704
www.wau.org

20 19 18 17 16 1 2 3 4

Nihil obstat: The Reverend Michael Morgan, J.D., J.C.L.
J.C.L Censor Librorum
October 26, 2016

Imprimatur: Most Reverend Felipe J. Estevez
Bishop of St. Augustine
October 26, 2016

ISBN: 978-1-59325-305-9
eISBN:978-1-59325-490-2

Scripture texts are taken from the Catholic Edition of the Revised Standard Version Bible, © 1965, 1966 by the Division of Christian Education of the National Council of the Churches of Christ in the United States of America. Used with permission. All rights reserved.

Excerpts from the English translation of the *Catechism of the Catholic Church* for use in the United States of America ©1994, United States Catholic Conference, Inc.—Libreria Editrice Vaticana.

Cover design by Andrea Alvarez

No part of this publication may be reproduced, stored in a retrieval system, or transmitted in any form or by any means—electronic, mechanical, photocopy, recording, or any other—except for brief quotations in printed reviews, without the prior permission of the author and publisher.

Made and printed in the United States of America

Library of Congress Control Number: 2016959638

Contents

Introduction

"Yet even now," says the LORD,
 "return to me with all your heart,
with fasting, with weeping, and with mourning;
 and rend your hearts and not your garments."
Return to the LORD, your God,
 for he is gracious and merciful,
slow to anger, and abounding in steadfast love,
 and repents of evil.

—Joel 2:12-13

The moment has come! The time is now! The hour is upon you regardless of your past mistakes or the difficulty of your current circumstances—or even if your spirit feels distant from God or your heart feels hardened. "Even now," the Lord calls, "return to me with all your heart."

God's plea is straightforward and simple: he wants you close to him. He yearns for you as a father or mother longs for a lost child. God is asking you to stop what you normally do and take the time this Lent to discover what he means in your life, and what he could mean.

The inner turbulence so many people experience today tells us that the promises of the world do not satisfy the deepest hungers of our hearts. We all repeat the same questions: "Why am I striving so hard? What am I searching for? How can I find true life, purpose, and fulfillment?" These thoughts persist because they cannot be answered without God or a relationship with Jesus that allows us to hear God's voice in his.

Jesus wants that relationship with you. This book will help you seek him as he is seeking you, by reflecting on the Lenten Sunday Mass readings, either alone or in a small group. If you enter in "with all your heart," you will be able to respond to Jesus' call to conversion. "This time is fulfilled, and the kingdom of God is at hand; repent, and believe in the gospel" (Mark 1:15). Those were the first words of Jesus as he began his public ministry. The biblical Greek for "repent" is *metanoia*, which means "change your mind and your heart." Conversion of heart is the core of the gospel.

Encountering Jesus makes that change possible. He can transform our hearts, if we let him in. The kingdom of God broke into the physical world through him in a completely new and unprecedented way. In Jesus the fullness of God became present, tangible, and accessible to you and the whole human family. And he is still with you: "And lo, I am with you always, to the close of the age" (Matthew 28:20). If you're part of a small group, he will be there: "For where two or three are gathered in my name, there am I in the midst of them" (18:20).

If we believe this is true, that the Lord has come, that the kingdom of God is at hand because Jesus is truly with us, then what else would we want to do but know him and grow close to him?

Reflecting on the Scriptures opens to us the reality of who Jesus is. Once we come to know his love—a love so great that he forgave the people who were crucifying him while they were doing it—we want to surrender our whole lives to him. He extends to us the love that forgave even those who crucified him on the cross. Seeking him, we find the mercy we crave and the grace to forgive others. Jesus heals not only our own hearts, but through us, sometimes even those of our enemies, our families, and our friends. He is our way to peace.

Jesus is also the corrective to any erroneous impressions we may have about God the Father: that God wants to punish or belittle us for wandering, or is a cold, distant superpower rather than a person who loves us. Through Jesus' relationship with his Father, we see that God is not a heavenly scorekeeper, tallying our mistakes and weighing them against our merits. Lent is not a time when God wants to chasten us for our guilt but a time when he wants to welcome us home, like the Father in the story of the prodigal son (Luke 15:11-32).

Coming home requires figuring out what it is that gets in our way from enjoying a loving relationship with God. The self-examination that Lent encourages breaks down the barriers that we don't even know are there in our hearts and minds. Then true communion becomes possible.

That's why a spiritually fruitful Lent requires more than giving up chocolate or coffee. Outward signs and rituals play a role: they help our inward transformation to happen and manifest that change in our lives. But the Lord says through Joel, "Rend your hearts and not your garments." That means dying to the tyranny of self and all that stymies our spiritual journey or undermines or inhibits full communion with our loving God.

We pray with the Church that the Liturgy of the Word will penetrate your heart in a new way this year, bearing fruit that will endure forever in the kingdom of God. The time is now. Return to the Lord with all your heart through Lenten penance, almsgiving, and prayer so that you can fully experience the joy of the resurrection this Easter.

How to Use This Small Group Guide

Welcome to *With Jesus to the Cross: Year A*, a small group guide to help you know Jesus of Nazareth more deeply and understand more fully what his death and resurrection mean in your life.

Weekly Sessions

The weekly sessions use the Sunday Mass readings for Lent to help you enter into the mystery of Christ's life, suffering, and resurrection, the source of our salvation.

Each session includes written opening and closing prayers, the Scripture passages to be discussed that week, questions for discussion, ideas for action, and prayer prompts to carry you through the week. Sometimes excerpts from saints, popes, or other great teachers are included that shed light on the message of the gospel.

The sessions in this guide are self-contained. If you or a friend attends for the first time in Week 3, there will be no need to "catch up." Anyone can just dive right in with the rest of the group. As with Lent, instead of building sequentially, the sessions deepen thematically, helping you engage more with Jesus and the cross little by little.

The more you take notes, jot down ideas or questions, underline verses in your Bible (if you bring one to your small group, which we recommend!), and refer back to the sessions of previous weeks, the more God has the opportunity to speak to you through the discussion and the ideas he places in your heart. As with any endeavor, the more you put in, the more you get back.

The best way to take advantage of each week's discussion is to carry the theme into your life by following the suggestions in the "Connection to the Cross This Week" section. These prayer prompts will allow Jesus to enlighten your heart and mind on both the challenges of Lent and the joy of the resurrection. If you're discussing the readings with a small group, the facilitator will give you the chance to share experiences from the previous week and talk about the recommendations for the upcoming week during each session.

Each weekly session includes Scripture passages for meditation on the theme of the Sunday readings for that week as well as the daily Mass readings for the coming week. You can find these in your Bible, online (biblegateway.com, usccb.org, and other sites), or use any of the popular free apps that feature the daily Mass readings, such as Laudate or iMissal. The entire New American Bible is available at the U.S. Conference of Catholic Bishops' website, usccb.org, as well as the daily readings, including an audio version (http://usccb.org/bible/readings-audio.cfm).

Appendices

Helpful appendices for both participants and facilitators supplement the weekly materials. Appendices A through C are for participants, and Appendices D through F are for group facilitators.

Prior to your first group meeting, please read Appendix A, "Small Group Discussion Guide." These guidelines will help every person in the group set a respectful tone that creates the space for encountering Christ together. This small group will differ from other discussion groups you may have experienced. Is it a lecture? No. A book club? No. Appendix A will help you understand what this small group is and how you can help seek a "Spirit-led" discussion. Every member is responsible for the quality of the group dynamics. This appendix will help you fulfill your role of being a supportive and involved group member.

Appendix B is a resource to enhance and deepen your relationship with Jesus. It encourages you to take the "1% Challenge": pray at least fifteen minutes each day. That may sound like a lot, but this appendix also provides a step-by-step guide on how to spend the time.

In Appendix C, you will find a guide to the Sacrament of Reconciliation, commonly known as Confession. This sacrament bridges the distance we might feel from God that results from a variety of causes, including unrepented sin. The Church encourages Catholics to receive this sacrament each Lent, but it is tremendously helpful to receive it even more frequently. If you want to grow closer to Jesus and experience great peace, the Sacrament of Reconciliation provides a fast track. This appendix will help alleviate any anxiety by leading you through the steps of preparing for and going to Confession. It also gives suggestions for online resources that will provide questions for a fruitful examination of conscience.

While Appendices A through C are important for small group participants and facilitators alike, Appendices D through F support the facilitators in their role. A facilitator is not a teacher. His or her role is to buoy the conversation, encourage fruitful group discussion, and tend to the group dynamics.

Appendix D provides guidance and best practices for facilitating a small group successfully, and includes recommendations for any difficult group dynamics that could arise. You will find guidelines on what makes a group work: building genuine friendships, calling for the Holy Spirit to be the group's true facilitator, and seeking joy together.

Appendix E takes the facilitator from the general to the specific, providing detailed leader notes for each session of *With Jesus to the Cross*. Read these notes four or five days before each group meeting. The notes will help you prepare each session by providing a "heads up" on the content and issues that pertain to discussing these particular Scripture passages.

Facilitators should read Appendix F well in advance of the first meeting. It has the guidance you need to lead prayer and encourage participation in prayer by group members. While the material in each session includes a suggested prayer, this is only support material. It's far better for the group spiritually to pray in their own words. Appendix F will help the facilitator make that happen.

Learning this skill is important. It will model for the group members how to talk to Jesus in their own words. Closing with extemporaneous prayer is an extremely valuable way to seal the time you have spent together by offering up the discoveries, questions, and joys of your conversation. Appendix F will help you guide your group from awkward beginnings to a deepening experience of talking to God.

Appendix F will also help the facilitator bring the "Connection to the Cross This Week" section into the discussion for each session. It provides concrete suggestions on how to encourage and support group members in their personal engagement with the topics discussed. The facilitator plays a key role in helping participants allow Jesus to become more and more the center of their lives.

Enjoy the adventure!

1st

Sunday of Lent

Step into the Desert

Then Jesus was led
up by the Spirit into
the wilderness.
—Matthew 4:1

Praying together in your own words is always more natural than reading something together. A few words are fine—try to make it simple and brief. You could ask the Lord's blessing on your time together or invite the Holy Spirit to guide your conversation, or you could just thank God for gathering you together to discuss the Lenten Scriptures. Begin and end the prayer with the Sign of the Cross, and you're ready to begin!

If that feels too difficult, one person should slowly read the following prayer aloud, and invite the others to pray along silently in their hearts.

In the name of the Father, and of the Son, and of the Holy Spirit.

All-powerful God,
Father of our Lord Jesus Christ,
by water and the Holy Spirit,
you freed us from sin
and gave us new life.

During this season of Lent,
send your Holy Spirit once again
to guide us into solitude and reflection.
Be with us through the desolation of the desert,
fortify us against the evil one,
and renew us in the living waters of Jesus.

Give us a courageous and resolute spirit,
a spirit of sobriety and humility,
that we might have eyes to see
the darkness within us
and the painful reality of our sin.

Wash us clean again, O Spirit,
And fill us with wonder and awe in your presence.

We ask this through Christ our Lord.
Amen.

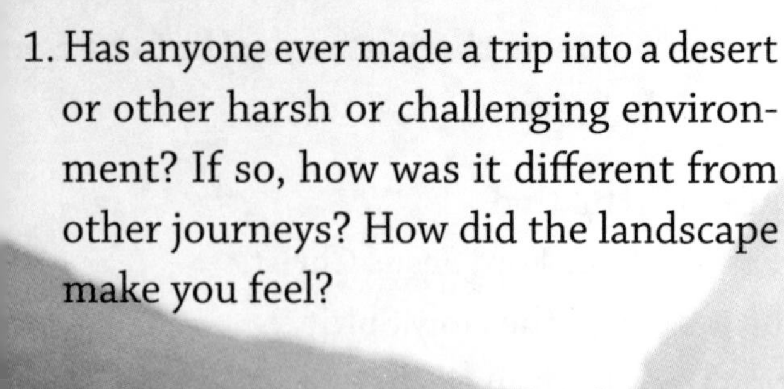

1. Has anyone ever made a trip into a desert or other harsh or challenging environment? If so, how was it different from other journeys? How did the landscape make you feel?

2. How are you preparing for the season of Lent?

Ask one person to read the following Scripture passage aloud.

Matthew 4:1-11

[1]Then Jesus was led up by the Spirit into the wilderness to be tempted by the devil. [2]And he fasted forty days and forty nights, and afterward he was hungry. [3]And the tempter came and said to him, "If you are the Son of God, command these stones to become loaves of bread." [4]But he answered, "It is written,

> 'Man shall not live by bread alone,
> but by every word that proceeds from the mouth of God.'"

[5]Then the devil took him to the holy city, and set him on the pinnacle of the temple, [6]and said to him, "If you are the Son of God, throw yourself down; for it is written,

> 'He will give his angels charge of you,'

and

> 'On their hands they will bear you up,
> lest you strike your foot against a stone.'"

[7]Jesus said to him, "Again it is written, 'You shall not tempt the Lord your God.'" [8]Again, the devil took him to a very high mountain, and showed him all the kingdoms of the world and the glory of them; [9]and he said to him, "All these I will give you, if you will fall down and worship me." [10]Then Jesus said to him, "Begone, Satan! for it is written,

> 'You shall worship the Lord your God
> and him only shall you serve.'"

[11]Then the devil left him, and behold, angels came and ministered to him.

1. What caught your attention in this passage?

2. According to verse 1, why did Jesus go to the desert?

3. Have you ever been in a "desert place" in which you were subject to temptations? What was that like?

4. The temptations Jesus faces can seem remote to our own lives. How could these temptations be relevant to your life today, especially when you find yourselves in a "desert place"?

5. How would you put into your own words what Jesus says to the devil in response to the first temptation (verse 4)?

6. How could you use the Scriptures to expose and overcome temptation? Has any particular Scripture verse been helpful in that regard?

7. After Jesus resists the devil the third time, what happens? What does this tell us about the journey of Lent?

Romans 5:12-19

12Therefore as sin came into the world through one man and
death through sin, and so death spread to all men because all men
sinned—13sin indeed was in the world before the law was given,
but sin is not counted where there is no law. 14Yet death reigned
from Adam to Moses, even over those whose sins were not like the
transgression of Adam, who was a type of the one who was to come.

15But the free gift is not like the trespass. For if many died
through one man's trespass, much more have the grace of God and
the free gift in the grace of that one man Jesus Christ abounded for
many. 16And the free gift is not like the effect of that one man's sin.
For the judgment following one trespass brought condemnation,
but the free gift following many trespasses brings justification.
17If, because of one man's trespass, death reigned through that
one man, much more will those who receive the abundance of
grace and the free gift of righteousness reign in life through the
one man Jesus Christ.

18Then as one man's trespass led to condemnation for all men,
so one man's act of righteousness leads to acquittal and life for all
men. 19For as by one man's disobedience many were made sinners,
so by one man's obedience many will be made righteous.

8. How would you say you've experienced the "abundance of grace" given through Jesus' life, death, and resurrection?

9. If you don't feel you've received that grace, how could you seek and claim what St. Paul says has been abundantly given in Christ?

If you have time, read the passage on the following page by Henri Nouwen, and reflect together on the questions. Ask one person to read the passage aloud. Otherwise, read it on your own and think about the questions before the next session. Review the "Connection to the Cross This Week" recommendations and close with prayer.

O Lord, . . . how often have I lived through these weeks of Lent without paying much attention to penance, fasting, and prayer? How often have I missed the spiritual fruits of this season without even being aware of it? But how can I ever really celebrate Easter without observing Lent? How can I rejoice fully in your resurrection when I have avoided participating in your death?

Yes, Lord, I have to die—with you, through you, and in you—and thus become ready to recognize you when you appear to me in your resurrection. There is so much in me that needs to die: false attachments, greed and anger, impatience and stinginess. O Lord, I am self-centered, concerned about myself, my career, my future, my name and fame. Often I even feel that I use you for my own advantage. How preposterous, how sacrilegious, how sad! But yes, Lord, I know it is true. . . . I see clearly now how little I have died with you, really gone your way and been faithful to it. O Lord, make this Lenten season different from the other ones. Let me find you again. Amen.

—Henri Nouwen[1]

[1] Henri Nouwen, *A Cry for Mercy: Prayers from the Genesee* (New York: Doubleday, 1983, 2002), p. 35.

1. What struck you from this passage?

2. Do any of Nouwen's sentiments feel familiar to you: things that are also true, in some way, in your life? How?

Take a few minutes of silence at home to privately reflect on the ways in which you are tempted or need to let go of any attachments to self-will, sin, or anything that is not of God. You may not recognize these at first. Ask the Holy Spirit to reveal them to you. Write them down in a journal or other private place.

Lent is a time when we can honestly assess our lives. The primary way we do this is in prayer. Time with the Lord allows God to help us examine our hearts and minds. He shows us where he wants us to grow, how he wants us to change, and the parts of ourselves we keep from him.

The question for Lent is not "What shall I do to improve myself?" but rather, "God, how do you want to make me more like you? I know I was made in your image, and can grow into your likeness through Jesus, but I also know that I don't always live as Jesus did. Help me see what needs to change, inside and out. I want to let the Holy Spirit into every part of my life." As St. Paul reminds us, "We all, with unveiled face, beholding the glory of the Lord, are being changed into his likeness from one degree of glory to another; for this comes from the Lord who is the Spirit" (2 Corinthians 3:18).

Only God knows the true condition of our hearts. Only God can help us see what we must overcome. The psalmist wisely prays, "Who can discern his errors? / Clear thou me from hidden faults" (19:12). If, by God's grace, we recognize our weaknesses, we still desperately need the power of God to change. Ultimately, only God, not even our best efforts, can triumph.

This week, commit to spending time in prayer. Find time slots in your calendar when you can spend fifteen to twenty minutes on at least two or, even better, three or four days. Then "close the door" of your room (cf. Matthew 6:6) and talk to God. Ask him to sow "truth in the inward being," the secret place where God can "teach [you] wisdom" (Psalm 51:6). Ask God to make you aware of the hidden faults in your life and to direct you toward the Lenten sacrifices that will truly lead you back to him.

Ask the Blessed Mother, Mary, to intercede for you, that you may be given the courage to see yourself clearly. Use the Scripture passages on the next page to help you reflect on your life, or use the daily Mass readings.

In prayer, make a commitment to the ways in which you will live the three pillars of Lent: prayer, fasting, and almsgiving. Creating time and space for prayer will itself require a little "fasting" from some other activity. Be open to the ways in which the Holy Spirit leads you to fast and give alms. Each week of this discussion guide will provide specific suggestions and Scripture passages for prayer.

Scripture Passages for Meditation:

- Psalm 51
- Romans 7:15-25
- Deuteronomy 7:25–8:5
- James 4:1-10
- 1 John 1:5-10
- John 20:19-23

This Week's Mass Readings:

Monday: Lv 19:1-2, 11-18 • Ps 19:8-10, 15 • Mt 25:31-46
Tuesday: Is 55:10-11 • Ps 34:4-7, 16-19 • Mt 6:7-15
Wednesday: Jon 3:1-10 • Ps 51:3-4, 12-13, 18-19 • Lk 11:29-32
Thursday: Est C:12, 14-16, 23-25 • Ps 138:1-3, 7-8 • Mt 7:7-12
Friday: Ez 18:21-28 • Ps 130:1-8 • Mt 5:20-26
Saturday: Dt 26:16-19 • Ps 119:1-2, 4-5, 7-8 • Mt 5:43-48

As with the opening prayer, praying in our own words best shares our hearts with God. Invite the group members to pray spontaneous prayers to the Lord. If that is too difficult, ask someone to close by reading the following prayer aloud slowly while the rest pray along silently.

In the Name of the Father, and of the Son, and of the Holy Spirit.

Lord of infinite compassion and steadfast love,
we stand before you in humility and trust.
Look with compassion on us as we acknowledge
our sinfulness.
Stretch out your hand to save us and raise us up
in your goodness.

Do not allow the power of darkness to triumph
over us,
but cleanse us from our faults.
As members of Christ's body,
we long to be sheep of your own flock.

We ask this through our Lord Jesus Christ,
your Son,
who lives and reigns with you and the Holy Spirit,
one God, for ever and ever.
Amen.

2nd Sunday of Lent

Strength for the Journey

And he was transfigured before them, and his face shone like the sun, and his garments became white as light.

—Matthew 17:2

Ask someone to pray in their own words, or read the following prayer aloud slowly as others pray along silently.

In the name of the Father, and of the Son, and of the Holy Spirit.

We praise you, O heavenly Father,
Father of our Lord Jesus Christ,
for you have promised to remember us.

"Lord God, holy Lover of our souls,
when you come into our hearts,
all that is within us shall rejoice.
"You are our glory and the exultation of our hearts;
you are our hope and refuge in the day of trouble."[1]

Enlighten our understanding as we read
and reflect on your word.
May your Holy Spirit guide our discussion.
Grant that through this time together,
we might know you more truly and
come to love you more fully.

We pray this through Christ our Lord.
Amen.

[1] Adapted from Thomas á Kempis, *Imitation of Christ*, Book 3, Chapter 5.

Describe a time when you were given something and could not repay the gift or favor. How did that make you feel?

Ask one person to read the following Scripture passage aloud.

Matthew 17:1-9

1And after six days Jesus took with him Peter and James and John his brother, and led them up a high mountain apart. 2And he was transfigured before them, and his face shone like the sun, and his garments became white as light. 3And behold, there appeared to them Moses and Elijah, talking with him. 4And Peter said to Jesus, "Lord, it is well that we are here; if you wish, I will make three booths here, one for you and one for Moses and one for Elijah." 5He was still speaking, when lo, a bright cloud overshadowed them, and a voice from the cloud said, "This is my beloved Son, with whom I am well pleased; listen to him." 6When the disciples heard this, they fell on their faces, and were filled with awe. 7But Jesus came and touched them, saying, "Rise, and have no fear." 8And when they lifted up their eyes, they saw no one but Jesus only.

9And as they were coming down the mountain, Jesus commanded them, "Tell no one the vision, until the Son of man is raised from the dead."

1. What strikes you most about this Scripture passage?

2. What were the various elements of the vision that Peter, James, and John experienced? How would you describe what the disciples saw?

3. This passage presents Moses and Elijah conversing with the transfigured Lord. In Jewish tradition, Moses represents the Law, and Elijah, the prophets. What does this add to your understanding of the significance of the transfiguration?

4. What ways did the disciples react to the vision? How does that compare to how you think you might react?

5. How do you think this vision affected the disciples, both immediately afterward and in the days to come in Jerusalem?

6. As a disciple of Christ, what hope or encouragement can you take from this Scripture passage?

7. How could Jesus' words to his disciples, "Rise, and have no fear" (verse 7), pertain to Lent?

Ask one person to read the following Scripture passage aloud.

2 Timothy 1:8-10

8 Do not be ashamed then of testifying to our Lord, nor of me his
prisoner, but take your share of suffering for the gospel in the
power of God, 9 who saved us and called us with a holy calling,
not in virtue of our works but in virtue of his own purpose and
the grace which he gave us in Christ Jesus ages ago, 10 and now
has manifested through the appearing of our Savior Christ Jesus,
who abolished death and brought life and immortality to light
through the gospel.

8. Paul tells Timothy that God saves us "not in virtue of our works but in virtue of his own purpose." Does this change or influence the way you view God, yourself, or your relationship with God? How?

9. What encouragement does this Scripture passage offer to us for Lent?

EXIT

God's free grace is most fully offered in the Eucharist at Mass. So freely does God give his very self that Catholics can easily take for granted this offering of intimacy with the Lord. Just as God chose Peter, James, and John to walk closely with him, so he chooses us. We enter into that intimacy in a special way when we receive the Eucharist mindfully and prayerfully.

Find at least one day this week to attend daily Mass. (Masstimes.org lists all the daily and Sunday Masses in many U.S. cities and towns.) Pray to experience Communion more fully, to be more closely united to Christ through this sacrament.

On the days you don't go to Mass, use the Scripture passages listed on page 37 for reflection or the daily Mass readings. Passages are provided each week because Scripture has the power to transform your life so completely. Praying with the word of God will help you hear what God has to say to you, individually and specifically.

This week, take the "1% Challenge": spend fifteen minutes of each day praying with Scripture. That's just 1% of your life—not all that much time, really, to give to the One who created you and loves you. (For more guidance on what to do in those fifteen minutes, see the "1% Challenge" in Appendix B, "A Guide to Seeking God in Prayer and Scripture." It shares methods that have helped Christians for the last two millennia to grow in love and knowledge of God.)

Praying with Scripture will allow the Holy Spirit to shape your life and help you hear the voice of God in your heart (see Romans 8:11). If you approach Scripture with a heart open to God's will, he will draw your attention to words or phrases as a means of introducing topics, feelings, transitions in your life, and a host of other things that he wants to talk to you about.

Every major Church teaching and Church leader promotes reading the Scriptures precisely because it is the primary means by which God communicates with us. It makes a type of intimacy with God possible that is available no other way. This is from the *Catechism of the Catholic Church*, which quotes Section 25 of the Second Vatican Council's document *Dei Verbum*:

> The Church "forcefully and specially exhorts all the Christian faithful . . . to learn 'the surpassing knowledge of Jesus Christ' (Philippians 3:8) by frequent reading of the divine Scriptures. . . . Let them remember, however, that prayer should accompany the reading of Sacred Scripture, so that a dialogue takes place between God and man. For 'we speak to him when we pray; we listen to him when we read the divine oracles' (St. Ambrose, *De officiis ministrorum*)." (2653)

And here is what Pope Benedict XVI said in his encyclical *Verbum Domini:*

> With the Synod Fathers I express my heartfelt hope for the flowering of "a new season of greater love for sacred Scripture on the part of every member of the People of God, so that their prayerful and faith-filled reading of the Bible will, with

> time, deepen their personal relationship with Jesus." (72) May the Lord himself, as in the time of the prophet Amos, raise up in our midst a new hunger and thirst for the word of God (cf. Amos 8:11). (91)

Take these words to heart! Make time to listen to the Lord this week through reading and praying with the Scriptures. Hearing from God will make you want more! Prayer begets prayer, generating that hunger for the Scriptures that Pope Benedict wants all Catholics to experience. Use the following Scripture passages or the daily Mass readings for prayer and reflection. If some other passages from Scripture beckon you, don't hesitate to pray with them instead. That is the Holy Spirit prompting your heart.

Scripture Passages for Meditation:

- Matthew 6:7-15
- Matthew 7:7-14
- Jeremiah 17:5-17
- Matthew 5:20-26
- Luke 16:19-31
- Matthew 5:43-48

This Week's Mass Readings:

Monday: Dn 9:4-10 • Ps 78:8-9, 11,13 • Lk 6:36-38

Tuesday: Is 1:10, 16-20 • Ps 50:8-9, 16-17, 21, 23 • Mt 23:1-12

Wednesday: Jer 18:18-20 • Ps 31:5-6, 14, 15-16 • Mt 20:17-28

Thursday: Jer 17:5-10 • Ps 1:1-4, 6 • Lk 16:19-31

Friday: Gn 37:3-4, 12-13, 17-28 • Ps 105:16-21 • Mt 21:33-43, 45-46

Saturday: Mi 7:14-15, 18-20 • Ps 103:1-4, 9-12 • Lk 15:1-3, 11-32

The facilitator or someone else should invite the group members to speak to God directly in brief spontaneous prayers, offering the first prayer to "prime the pump." Once there is silence again, invite the group to pray together the psalm below. The group could read the psalm antiphonally, as monastics do, with half the group praying one stanza and the other half reading the next stanza. Continue alternating until the end. Before you begin, make sure everyone in the group understands how you will transition from the extemporaneous prayer to the psalm.

In the name of the Father, and of the Son, and of the Holy Spirit.

I will extol thee, my God and King,
  and bless thy name for ever and ever.
Every day I will bless thee,
  and praise thy name for ever and ever.
Great is the LORD, and greatly to be praised,
  and his greatness is unsearchable. . .

The LORD is faithful in all his words,
  and gracious in all his deeds.
The LORD upholds all who are falling,
  and raises up all who are bowed down.

The eyes of all look to thee,
  and thou gives them their food in due season.
Thou opens thy hand,
  thou satisfies the desire of every living thing.

The LORD is just in all his ways,
  and kind in all his doings.
The LORD is near to all who call upon him,
  to all who call upon him in truth.

He fulfills the desire of all who fear him,
  he also hears their cry, and saves them.
The LORD preserves all who love him;
  but all the wicked he will destroy.

My mouth will speak the praise of the LORD,
  and let all flesh bless his holy name for ever and ever.
(Psalm 145:1-3, 13b-21)

Amen.

3rd Sunday of Lent
Experience Living Water

"If you knew the gift of God,
. . . you would have asked him,
and he would have given you
living water."

—John 4:10

Ask someone to pray in their own words, or read aloud the following prayer slowly as others pray along silently.

In the name of the Father, and of the Son, and of the Holy Spirit.

Lord Jesus,
Your love reaches out in mercy
to embrace and heal the contrite of heart.

Lead us along the way of holiness,
and heal the wounds of our sins.

May we always keep safe in all its fullness
the gift of your love.

Let your mercy now restore us,
for you are Lord of all forever and ever.

Amen.

What comes to mind when you hear the word "water"? Does it evoke life or death, recreation or hardship, fear or delight?

Ask one person to read the following Scripture passage aloud.

John 4:5-26

5So he came to a city of Samaria, called Sychar, near
the field that Jacob gave to his son Joseph. 6Jacob's
well was there, and so Jesus, wearied as he was with
his journey, sat down beside the well. It was about
the sixth hour.

7There came a woman of Samaria to draw water.
Jesus said to her, "Give me a drink." 8For his disciples
had gone away into the city to buy food. 9The Samaritan woman said to him, "How is it that you, a Jew,
ask a drink of me, a woman of Samaria?" For Jews
have no dealings with Samaritans. 10Jesus answered
her, "If you knew the gift of God, and who it is that is
saying to you, 'Give me a drink,' you would have asked
him, and he would have given you living water." 11The
woman said to him, "Sir, you have nothing to draw
with, and the well is deep; where do you get that living
water? 12Are you greater than our father Jacob, who
gave us the well, and drank from it himself, and his
sons, and his cattle?" 13Jesus said to her, "Every one
who drinks of this water will thirst again, 14but whoever drinks of the water that I shall give him will never

thirst; the water that I shall give him will become in him a spring
of water welling up to eternal life." 15 The woman said to him, "Sir,
give me this water, that I may not thirst, nor come here to draw."
16 Jesus said to her, "Go, call your husband, and come here."
17 The woman answered him, "I have no husband." Jesus said to
her, "You are right in saying, 'I have no husband'; 18 for you have
had five husbands, and he whom you now have is not your husband; this you said truly." 19 The woman said to him, "Sir, I perceive
that you are a prophet. 20 Our fathers worshiped on this mountain; and you say that in Jerusalem is the place where men ought
to worship." 21 Jesus said to her, "Woman, believe me, the hour is
coming when neither on this mountain nor in Jerusalem will you
worship the Father. 22 You worship what you do not know; we worship what we know, for salvation is from the Jews. 23 But the hour
is coming, and now is, when the true worshipers will worship the
Father in spirit and truth, for such the Father seeks to worship
him. 24 God is spirit, and those who worship him must worship in
spirit and truth." 25 The woman said to him, "I know that Messiah
is coming (he who is called Christ); when he comes, he will show
us all things." 26 Jesus said to her, "I who speak to you am he."

1. What happens in this interaction between Jesus and the Samaritan woman? How does it begin? What is said?

2. What traditions and social customs of the day make this interaction unlikely? Why is this encounter so surprising?

3. Have you ever experienced being surprised by an encounter with Jesus? If so, are you willing to share it?

Ask a different person to read aloud the next section of the Scripture passage.

John 4:27-42

27 Just then his disciples came. They marveled that he was talking
with a woman, but none said, "What do you wish?" or, "Why are
you talking with her?" 28 So the woman left her water jar, and went
away into the city, and said to the people, 29 "Come, see a man who
told me all that I ever did. Can this be the Christ?" 30 They went out
of the city and were coming to him.

31 Meanwhile the disciples besought him, saying, "Rabbi,
eat." 32 But he said to them, "I have food to eat of which you
do not know." 33 So the disciples said to one another, "Has any
one brought him food?" 34 Jesus said to them, "My food is to
do the will of him who sent me, and to accomplish his work.
35 Do you not say, 'There are yet four months, then comes the
harvest'? I tell you, lift up your eyes, and see how the fields
are already white for harvest. 36 He who reaps receives wages,
and gathers fruit for eternal life, so that sower and reaper
may rejoice together. 37 For here the saying holds true, 'One
sows and another reaps.' 38 I sent you to reap that for which
you did not labor; others have labored, and you have entered
into their labor."

39 Many Samaritans from that city believed in him because
of the woman's testimony, "He told me all that I ever did."
40 So when the Samaritans came to him, they asked him to
stay with them; and he stayed there two days. 41 And many
more believed because of his word. 42 They said to the woman,
"It is no longer because of your words that we believe, for we

have heard for ourselves, and we know that this is indeed the Savior of the world."

4. According to verse 28, what did the Samaritan woman do after encountering Jesus? What did she leave behind?

5. Peter and Andrew left their nets. James and John left their boat. Matthew left his tax stall. The woman at the well likewise left something behind. What is the significance of those items? What do they represent in the lives of these disciples?

6. Do you feel you've ever left anything behind in order to follow Jesus more closely?

7. Could Jesus be calling you to leave something behind this Lent? Is anyone willing to share about that?

8. After her encounter with Jesus, where did the Samaritan woman go? What did she do? What do you think motivated her, and what does that say to us today?

9. What reaction did she receive? Why did others in the town believe her? What gave them a firm and final belief that Jesus was truly the Messiah and Savior?

10. Reflect on your own faith in Jesus. Why do you believe that he is the Son of God and Savior of the world?

Take some time this week to think about your belief in God: where it came from, where it is going, and where you hope it is going. Who was the person who first told you the story of Jesus Christ? Who showed you, by the way they lived their lives, the transformative presence of God? Thank God for the loving obedience of those disciples, for extending to you what they had experienced in Christ.

This week, pray for the people in your life who have never experienced the love of God through the Church or the people of God. Pray for each person individually; spend time lifting each one of them up to the Lord.

After you've prayed for someone, ask God if there is some way you can show his love to that person. God will know if he or she needs something in particular that you can do. If nothing emerges in prayer, plan some small loving act that you think the person would appreciate, even if it is just a phone call. With our busy lives, we sometimes neglect friends and family for too long. (A social media post or text message doesn't count!)

Toward the end of the week, ask the Lord if any of these people are ready to hear more about him from you. Jesus knows who would be receptive to your authentic personal witness about how God's presence in your life has helped and blessed you. This can be very simple; for example, you might share a short witness in response to someone's expression of worry or concern for a loved one: "It really helps me to give my worries to Jesus. He said not to worry. I know he will carry my worries for me when I ask him to."

Ask God to create opportunities for you to share your experiences of him and to show you the opportunities he is creating.

Use the Scripture passages below or the daily Mass readings for prayer and reflection this week.

Scripture Passages for Meditation:

- Mark 1:16-20
- Luke 5:1-11
- Luke 24:13-35
- 1 John 1:1-4
- Luke 9:57-62
- Hebrews 13:7

This Week's Mass Readings:

Monday: 2 Kg 5:1-15 • Ps 42:2-3; 43:3-4 • Lk 4:24-30
Tuesday: Dn 3:25, 34-43 • Ps 25:4-9 • Mt 18:21-35
Wednesday: Dt 4:1, 5-9 • Ps 147:12-13, 15-16, 19-20 • Mt 5:17-19
Thursday: Jer 7:23-28 • Ps 95:1-2, 6-9 • Lk 11:14-23
Friday: Hos 14:2-10 • Ps 81:6-11, 14, 17 • Mark 12:28-34
Saturday: Hos 6:1-6 • Ps 51:3-4, 18-21 • Luke 18:9-14

The facilitator or a volunteer should open the shared prayer by praying first about what was discussed during the meeting and then inviting others to do the same. Afterward, the facilitator or whoever opens the shared prayer can read aloud the following prayer as others pray along silently.

In the name of the Father, and of the Son, and of the Holy Spirit.

Lord God,
Your love brings us life
and your mercy gives us new birth.
Look favorably upon us
during this season of Lent.

Reveal yourself to us more deeply,
as you did for the woman at the well.
As you did for her, change us.
Conform our lives to the pattern
of Christ's faithfulness.

May Jesus become our living water,
and may we experience today
the eternal power flowing from our baptism.
We pray this through Christ, our Lord.

Amen.

4th
Sunday of Lent
Live in the Light

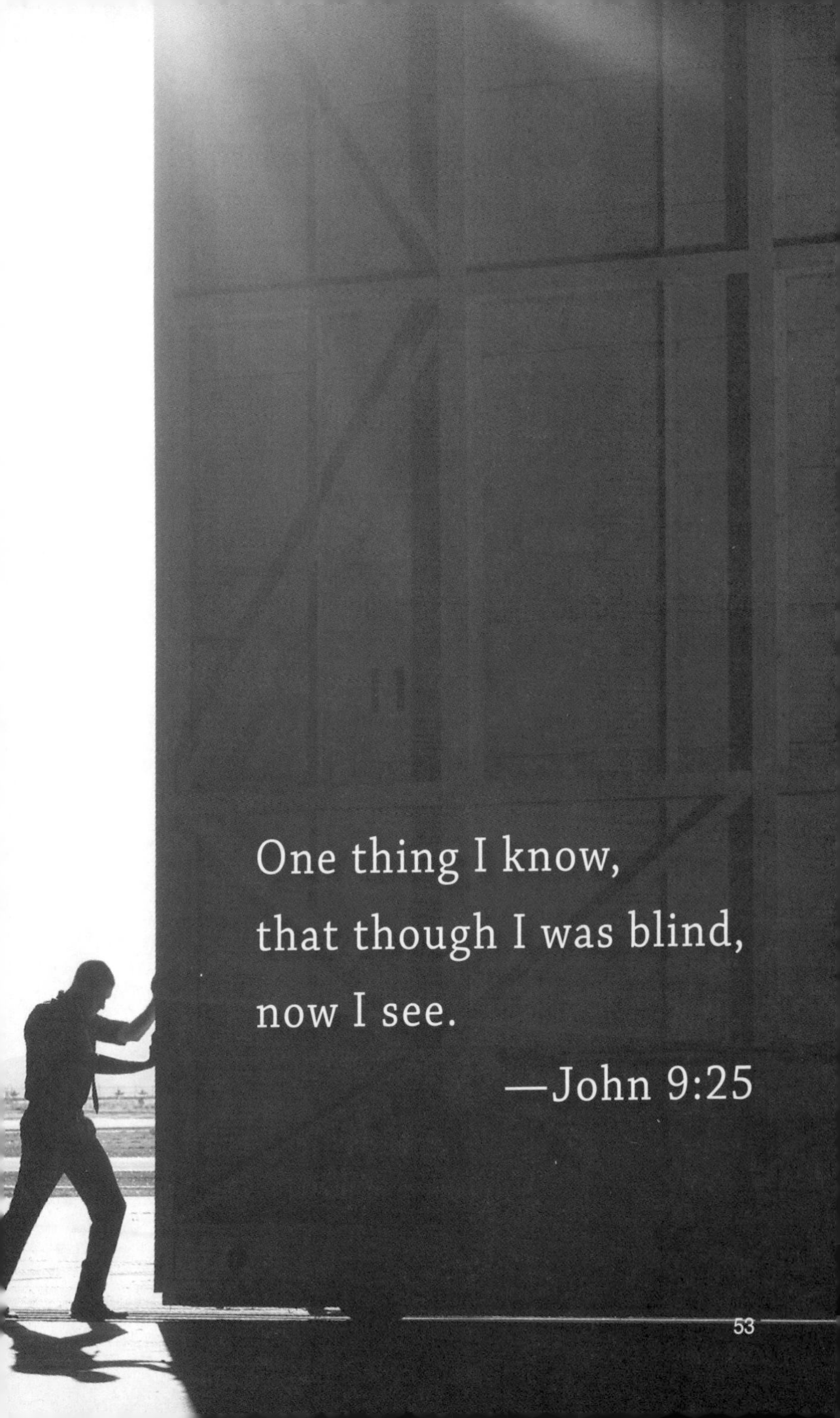

One thing I know,
that though I was blind,
now I see.

—John 9:25

Ask someone to pray in their own words, or read aloud the following prayer slowly as others pray along silently.

In the name of the Father, and of the Son, and of the Holy Spirit.

Let us pause before we pray together and recall God's constant presence with us throughout our day.

(Brief pause)

Father of light,
In you is found no shadow of change
but only the fullness of life and limitless truth.

Open our hearts to the voice of your Word,
and free us from the original darkness that shadows our vision.

Restore our sight that we may look upon your Son
who calls us to repentance and a change of heart.[1]

Grant us your Holy Spirit to dwell with us,
and inspire us as we gather together,
through Christ Jesus, our Lord.

Amen.

[1] Alternate opening prayer for the Second Sunday of Lent.

Briefly describe your experience of the Sacrament of Reconciliation. Has it been liberating? Intimidating? Eye-opening? Helpful?

Ask four members of the group to each read one of the following Scripture passages aloud.

John 9:1-17, 24-41

Reader 1

[1]As he passed by, he saw a man blind from his
birth. [2]And his disciples asked him, "Rabbi,
who sinned, this man or his parents, that he
was born blind?" [3]Jesus answered, "It was not
that this man sinned, or his parents, but that
the works of God might be made manifest in
him. [4]We must work the works of him who
sent me, while it is day; night comes, when no
one can work. [5]As long as I am in the world,
I am the light of the world." [6]As he said this,
he spat on the ground and made clay of the
spittle and anointed the man's eyes with the
clay, [7]saying to him, "Go, wash in the pool of
Siloam" (which means Sent). So he went and
washed and came back seeing. [8]The neighbors
and those who had seen him before as a beg-
gar, said, "Is not this the man who used to
sit and beg?" [9]Some said, "It is he"; others
said, "No, but he is like him." He said, "I am

the man." [10]They said to him, "Then how were your eyes
opened?" [11]He answered, "The man called Jesus made clay
and anointed my eyes and said to me, 'Go to Siloam and
wash'; so I went and washed and received my sight." [12]They
said to him, "Where is he?" He said, "I do not know."

Reader 2

[13]They brought to the Pharisees the man who had formerly
been blind. [14]Now it was a sabbath day when Jesus made
the clay and opened his eyes. [15]The Pharisees again asked
him how he had received his sight. And he said to them,
"He put clay on my eyes, and I washed, and I see." [16]Some
of the Pharisees said, "This man is not from God, for he
does not keep the sabbath." But others said, "How can a
man who is a sinner do such signs?" There was a division
among them. [17]So they again said to the blind man, "What
do you say about him, since he has opened your eyes?" He
said, "He is a prophet.". . .

Reader 3

[24]So for the second time they called the man who had been
blind, and said to him, "Give God the praise; we know that
this man is a sinner." [25]He answered, "Whether he is a sinner, I do not know; one thing I know, that though I was
blind, now I see." [26]They said to him, "What did he do to
you? How did he open your eyes?" [27]He answered them,
"I have told you already, and you would not listen. Why
do you want to hear it again? Do you too want to become
his disciples?" [28]And they reviled him, saying, "You are his
disciple, but we are disciples of Moses. [29]We know that God

has spoken to Moses, but as for this man, we do not know
where he comes from." 30The man answered, "Why, this is
a marvel! You do not know where he comes from, and yet
he opened my eyes. 31We know that God does not listen
to sinners, but if any one is a worshiper of God and does
his will, God listens to him. 32Never since the world began
has it been heard that any one opened the eyes of a man
born blind. 33If this man were not from God, he could do
nothing." 34They answered him, "You were born in utter
sin, and would you teach us?" And they cast him out.

Reader 4

35Jesus heard that they had cast him out, and having
found him he said, "Do you believe in the Son of man?"
36He answered, "And who is he, sir, that I may believe in
him?" 37Jesus said to him, "You have seen him, and it is
he who speaks to you." 38He said, "Lord, I believe"; and he
worshiped him. 39Jesus said, "For judgment I came into this
world, that those who do not see may see, and that those
who see may become blind." 40Some of the Pharisees near
him heard this, and they said to him, "Are we also blind?"
41Jesus said to them, "If you were blind, you would have no
guilt; but now that you say, 'We see,' your guilt remains."

1. What strikes you about this story?

2. The man born blind makes a variety of statements about Jesus throughout the narrative (see verses 11, 17, 25, 27, 30, 33, and 38; you may want to underline them in your booklet or Bible). Take a moment to note them all. **(Pause.)** What do these statements indicate about the blind man's experience of being healed by Jesus?

3. The Pharisees, or "the Jews,"[1] interrogate the man born blind. Take a moment to note the various statements they make (see verses 16, 24, 28-29, 34, and 40). **(Pause.)** How would you characterize them based on the progression of their interrogations?

4. Based on your observations above, compare and contrast the progression of the Pharisees' and blind man's ideas about Jesus.

5. Chapter 9 of the Gospel of John served as a reading to prepare converts for baptism in the early Church.[2] Why do you think the Church used this passage as baptismal catechesis?

[1] John 9:18 (not included here) uses the term "the Jews" to indicate the Jewish leaders. The term is also used elsewhere in St. John's Gospel. Jesus, his mother, and his brothers were Jews, as were all of his followers. The authorities interrogate the man born blind, not everyone in the town. The ruling religious and political leaders are the ones who are concerned about Jesus' activities.

[2] Raymond E. Brown, *The Gospel According to John I–XII (Anchor Bible Series)* (Garden City, NY: Doubleday, 1966), p. 380.

6. What does the physical healing of the man born blind symbolize for us with regard to the spiritual life?

7. In verse 39, Jesus reveals a deeper meaning of his healing of the man born blind. How would you explain what he is saying?

8. In verse 41, Jesus says to the Pharisees, "If you were blind, you would have no guilt; but now that you say, 'We see,' your guilt remains." How do you understand the meaning of Jesus' concluding statement to the Pharisees?

9. Can you identify past obstacles in your life that made you spiritually blind and hindered gospel living? What helped you to see your own spiritual blindness?

10. The man born blind said to Jesus, "Lord, I believe," and he worshiped Jesus. "Lord, I believe" is a confession of our baptism or a desire for baptism. What spiritual habits help you to renew your confession, or perhaps make it for the first time?

If time allows, you could read the passage from Pope Francis in "Connection to the Cross This Week" and discuss the questions.

Early in the week before your next small group meeting, read this excerpt from Pope Francis and consider that follow.

Through the Sacraments of Christian Initiation—Baptism, Confirmation, and the Eucharist —man receives new life in Christ. Now, we all know that we carry this life "in earthen vessels" (2 Corinthians 4:7), [so] we are still subject to temptation, suffering, and death and, because of sin, we may even lose this new life. That is why the Lord Jesus willed that the Church continue his saving work even to her own members, especially through the Sacrament of Reconciliation and the Anointing of the Sick, which can be united under the heading of "Sacraments of Healing." The Sacrament of Reconciliation is a sacrament of healing. When I go to Confession, it is in order to be healed, to heal my soul, to heal my heart, and to be healed of some wrongdoing. . . .

The Sacrament of Penance and Reconciliation flows directly from the Paschal Mystery. . . . [F]orgiveness of our sins is not something we can give ourselves. I cannot say: I forgive my sins. Forgiveness is asked for, is asked of another, and in Confession we ask for forgiveness from Jesus. Forgiveness is not the fruit of our own efforts but rather a gift; it is a gift of the Holy Spirit who fills us with the wellspring of mercy and of grace that flows unceasingly from the open heart of the

Crucified and Risen Christ. . . . [W]e can truly be at peace only if we allow ourselves to be reconciled, in the Lord Jesus, with the Father and with the brethren. And we have all felt this in our hearts, when we have gone to Confession with a soul weighed down and with a little sadness; and when we receive Jesus' forgiveness, we feel at peace, with that peace of soul which is so beautiful, and which only Jesus can give, only Him. . . .

In fact, the Christian community is the place where the Spirit is made present, who renews hearts in the love of God and makes all of the brethren one thing in Christ Jesus. . . . . In the celebration of this Sacrament, the priest represents not only God but also the whole community, who sees itself in the weakness of each of its members, who listens and is moved by his repentance, and who is reconciled with him, which cheers him up and accompanies him on the path of conversion and human and Christian growth. . . .

Dear friends, celebrating the Sacrament of Reconciliation means being enfolded in a warm embrace: it is the embrace of the Father's infinite mercy. . . . I am telling you: each time we go to Confession, God embraces us. God rejoices![1]

—General Audience, February 19, 2014

[1] Accessed at http://w2.vatican.va/content/francesco/en/audiences/2014/documents/papa-francesco_20140219_udienza-generale.html.

1. What from this reflection struck you?

2. Does anything hinder you from celebrating the Sacrament of Reconciliation?

3. Has anything helped you to receive this sacrament with more faith and less anxiety? What was it, and how did it help?

4. How can Pope Francis' words increase your faith and courage in receiving this sacrament?

Plan a time this week to celebrate the Sacrament of Reconciliation. Beforehand, read and consider Appendix C for helpful tips. Give the Holy Spirit time to show you what you need to discuss with the priest.

If they are offered in your area, attend the Stations of the Cross on Friday this week, or mark your calendar for a Friday before Easter when you can attend. Consider inviting a friend or family member to go with you. Extended focus on the events of the crucifixion will enrich your Lenten prayer by helping you enter into Jesus' experience.

If you are unable to attend in person, you might consider using the prayers of the Stations of the Cross for your daily meditation. For a rich reflection, search online for "Stations of the Cross at the Colosseum by Pope John Paul II." However, simply contemplating each station in your heart may be more effective, depending on how you best pray.

Use the Scripture passages below or the daily Mass readings for prayer and reflection this week.

Scripture Passages for Meditation:

- Ephesians 5:8-14
- 2 Kings 5:1-15
- Matthew 18:21-35
- Luke 11:14-23
- Mark 12:28-34
- Luke 18:9-14 or Hosea 6:1-6

This Week's Mass Readings:

Monday: Is 65:17-21 • Ps 30:2, 4-6, 11-13 • John 4:43-54
Tuesday: Ez 47:1-9, 12 • Ps 46:2-3, 5-6, 8-9 • John 5:1-16
Wednesday: Is 49:8-15 • Ps 145:8-9, 13-14, 17-18 • John 5:17-30
Thursday: Ex 32:7-14 • Ps 106:19-23 • Jn 5:31-47
Friday: Wis 2:1, 12-22 • Ps 34:17-23 • Jn 7:1-2, 10, 25-30
Saturday: Jer 11:18-20 • Ps 7:2-3, 9-12 • Jn 7:40-53

If everyone in the group is already baptized, ask one person to lead the group in the renewal of their baptismal promises. Before you pray, spend time offering prayers of petition, thanksgiving, praise, or confession. When it seems that the group is ready to close, the leader should begin asking the questions. The group should respond with a heartfelt "I do" to each promise.

If any group members aren't baptized, someone should open extemporaneous prayer and invite the rest of the group to voice their prayers aloud as well. Close with the Our Father.

In the name of the Father, and of the Son, and of the Holy Spirit.

Leader

- Do you reject Satan? **(I do.)**
- And all his works?
- And all his empty promises?
- Do you believe in God, the Father Almighty, Creator of heaven and earth?
- Do you believe in Jesus Christ, his only Son, our Lord, who was born of the Virgin Mary, was crucified, died, and was buried, rose from the dead, and is now seated at the right hand of the Father?
- Do you believe in the Holy Spirit, the holy Catholic Church, the communion of saints, the forgiveness of sins, the resurrection of the body, and life everlasting?

God, the all-powerful Father of our Lord Jesus Christ, has given us a new birth by water and the Holy Spirit and has forgiven all our sins. May he also keep us faithful to our Lord Jesus Christ forever and ever.

All | **Amen.**

5th
Sunday of Lent
A Matter of Life and Death

"I am the resurrection and the life; he who believes in me, though he die, yet shall he live."

—John 11:25

Opening Prayer
Fifth Sunday of Lent

Ask someone to pray in their own words, and then read aloud the prayer below slowly as others pray along silently.

In the name of the Father, and of the Son, and of the Holy Spirit.

Dear God,
Sometimes you seem far away,
especially in times of trial.
We struggle to believe you hear us,
that you care.
We fear we are suffering alone.

Give us great hope, Jesus, that when death comes,
we will meet you face-to-face.
But also, Lord, help us know that
you are with us even now,
bringing "grace upon grace."[1]

[1] John 1:16: "And from his fullness have we all received, grace upon grace."

We need you, Jesus,
to raise us up from our daily deaths.
We need you to live the life you died to give us.

Holy Spirit, dwell in us so wholly
that our eyes may see, like the man born blind;
that our hearts will feel,
as Jesus felt for Lazarus and his sisters.
Help us live life to the fullest.[2]

Jesus, you seek us.
Help us seek you daily
so that during this life on earth,
eternal life will not be something
distant and irrelevant,
but rather our daily bread.

We ask this through Christ our Lord.
Amen.

[2] John 10:10b: "I came that they may have life, and have it abundantly."

Has anyone ever experienced a brush with death, when you weren't sure you were going to make it? How did you feel afterward? Did it change anything in your life?

Ask one person to read the following Scripture passage aloud.

Romans 8:8-11

8 [T]hose who are in the flesh cannot please God. 9But
you are not in the flesh, you are in the Spirit, if the
Spirit of God really dwells in you. Any one who does
not have the Spirit of Christ does not belong to him.
10But if Christ is in you, although your bodies are
dead because of sin, your spirits are alive because of
righteousness. 11If the Spirit of him who raised Jesus
from the dead dwells in you, he who raised Christ Jesus
from the dead will give life to your mortal bodies also
through his Spirit who dwells in you.

1. How do you experience God's Spirit dwelling within you? Does the Holy Spirit inside you seem real to you, or is it more of an abstract idea?

2. Has anyone had an experience when you felt you had received God's Spirit in a new way? What was that like?

3. If you have not had that experience, have you seen someone else go through a transformation so complete that it seemed as though God had put his Spirit into that person in a new way? How would you describe the change you saw in that person's life?

4. Do you seek the Spirit so that he can transform your life? How? If not, how could you go about that?

Ask three members of the group to each read one paragraph aloud from this excerpt from John 11:1-45, the story of Jesus raising Lazarus from the dead.

John 11:17-45

Reader 1:

> [17]Now when Jesus came, he found that Lazarus had already been in the tomb four days. [18]Bethany was near Jerusalem, about two miles off, [19]and many of the Jews had come to Martha and Mary to console them concerning their brother. [20]When Martha heard that Jesus was coming, she went and met him, while Mary sat in the house. [21]Martha said to Jesus, "Lord, if you had been here, my brother would not have died. [22]And even now I know that whatever you ask from God, God will give you." [23]Jesus said to her, "Your brother will rise again." [24]Martha said to him, "I know that he will rise again in the resurrection at the last day." [25]Jesus said to her, "I am the resurrection and the life; he who believes in me, though he die, yet shall

he live, 26and whoever lives and believes in me shall never
die. Do you believe this?" 27She said to him, "Yes, Lord; I
believe that you are the Christ, the Son of God, he who is
coming into the world."

Reader 2:

28When she had said this, she went and called her sister
Mary, saying quietly, "The Teacher is here and is calling for
you." 29And when she heard it, she rose quickly and went to
him. 30Now Jesus had not yet come to the village, but was
still in the place where Martha had met him. 31When the
Jews who were with her in the house, consoling her, saw
Mary rise quickly and go out, they followed her, suppos-
ing that she was going to the tomb to weep there. 32Then
Mary, when she came where Jesus was and saw him, fell
at his feet, saying to him, "Lord, if you had been here,
my brother would not have died." 33When Jesus saw her
weeping, and the Jews who came with her also weeping,
he was deeply moved in spirit and troubled; 34and he said,
"Where have you laid him?" They said to him, "Lord, come
and see." 35Jesus wept. 36So the Jews said, "See how he loved
him!" 37But some of them said, "Could not he who opened
the eyes of the blind man have kept this man from dying?"

Reader 3:

38Then Jesus, deeply moved again, came to the tomb; it
was a cave, and a stone lay upon it. 39Jesus said, "Take
away the stone." Martha, the sister of the dead man, said
to him, "Lord, by this time there will be an odor, for he
has been dead four days." 40Jesus said to her, "Did I not

> tell you that if you would believe you would see the glory
> of God?" 41So they took away the stone. And Jesus lifted
> up his eyes and said, "Father, I thank thee that thou hast
> heard me. 42I knew that thou hearest me always, but I
> have said this on account of the people standing by, that
> they may believe that thou didst send me." 43When he
> had said this, he cried with a loud voice, "Lazarus, come
> out." 44The dead man came out, his hands and feet bound
> with bandages, and his face wrapped with a cloth. Jesus
> said to them, "Unbind him, and let him go."
>
> 45Many of the Jews therefore, who had come with Mary
> and had seen what he did, believed in him.

5. Did anything strike you from this reading? Did you notice anything that you hadn't in the past?

6. How do you think Martha and Mary felt when they met Jesus after Lazarus had died? What do their words indicate (verses 21 and 32)? Have you ever experienced a similar feeling in your relationship with Jesus? How did you deal with that?

7. Why do you think Jesus is "deeply moved in spirit" and "troubled" (verse 33) to the point of weeping after he talks to Mary and Martha? What could have grieved his heart so much, even though it seems that he planned to raise Lazarus from the dead all along?

8. What lessons can we find in the fact that Jesus is weeping with his friends in their pain?

9. Why do you think Jesus wanted to raise Lazarus from the dead? Why wouldn't his own resurrection be enough to show future generations of followers that "death no longer has dominion" (Romans 6:9)?

10. One of the most fearful and awesome realities of life is that it ends. Death looms for every one of us, yet some people avoid, as much as possible, seeing it or thinking about it. Some have so much fear that they won't even visit facilities for the ill and aging. How does this story of Lazarus, Martha, and Mary affect your feelings about death?

Jesus said to her, "I am the resurrection and the life; he who believes in me, though he die, yet shall he live, and whoever lives and believes in me shall never die. Do you believe this?"

(John 11:25-26)

"Do you believe this?" Jesus asks Martha, and she declares that he is "the Christ, the Son of God" (John 11:27). To know who Jesus is, you don't have to be Peter, the rock on which God built the Church (Mark 8:27-30). Just an ordinary person like Martha, someone loved by Jesus who loves him in return, can see the truth. She knows he has power over death even before he raises Lazarus.

Jesus asks you the same question: "Do you believe this?"

This week, ask God to enlighten the eyes of your heart (cf. Ephesians 1:18) to see more clearly what Jesus means in your life. Ask him to increase your faith so that you can say with Martha, "You are the Christ, the Son of God."

Then ask God to show you what within you still needs to die this Lent for you to rise anew with Jesus at Easter. Could fear or anxiety, hurt or bitterness, or greed or jealousy be governing your thoughts and behaviors, instead of your faith in Jesus and your trust in what he teaches? If you haven't yet celebrated the Sacrament of Reconciliation this Lent, bring any areas that God shows you to Confession. Ask for the grace to let go of whatever keeps you from the love of Jesus.

Prepare your heart for Holy Week by devoting yourself to reading Scripture. On four days this week, set aside at least fifteen minutes—only 1% of your day—to pray and read the Scriptures. (See Appendix B for more guidance.) Praying with Scripture will transform your heart and help you experience the Spirit within you more profoundly.

God can change your life, heal your wounds, and open your heart, if you give him the time to do it. If you haven't yet devoted time to praying with Scripture, make it happen this week. God is always wooing those who move toward his love. Make the commitment. Pull out your calendar right now and write down the four different days and times when you will spend fifteen minutes praying with Scripture. Or set your alarm for twenty minutes earlier every day and do it then. Try reading the selected passages below or the daily Mass readings. Make time for God, and unspeakable riches will unfold.

Scripture Passages for Meditation:

- Luke 9:23-27
- Romans 8:1-13
- Psalm 51
- 1 Peter 4:12-19
- Matthew 28:1-20

This Week's Mass Readings:

Monday: Dn 13:1-9, 15-17, 19-30, 33-62 • Ps 23:1-6 • Jn 8:1-11
Tuesday: Nm 21:4-9 • Ps 102:2-3, 16-21 • Jn 8:21-30
Wednesday: Dn 3:14-20, 91-92, 95 • (Ps) Dn 3:52-56 • Jn 8:31-42
Thursday: Gn 17:3-9 • Ps 105:4-9 • Jn 8:51-59
Friday: Jer 20:10-13 • Ps 18:2-7 • Jn 10:31-42
Saturday: Ez 37:21-28 • (Ps) Jer 31:10-13 • Jn 11:45-56

Ask someone to lead the group in a time of extemporaneous prayer. When people are done praying in their own words, the leader may close the time by praying in his or her own words, or by reading the prayer below.

In the name of the Father, and of the Son, and of the Holy Spirit.

Lord, you wept for your friend Lazarus.
Make our hearts like yours,
full of love and compassion,
deeply moved by the sorrow of the death and decay
that is our lot in this life.

Lord, you died on a cross for us,
that we may have life.
You said we, too, must lose our lives to save them.
Help us to see where we need to die to ourselves:
ways we are selfish and self-absorbed,
when we have hardened our hearts to the
suffering all around us.

Through your Holy Spirit
give us new hearts and new minds.
Revive our spirits
as you revived Lazarus.
Help us to live as you lived,
and love as you loved.

Amen.

Palm Sunday

The Passion of the Lord

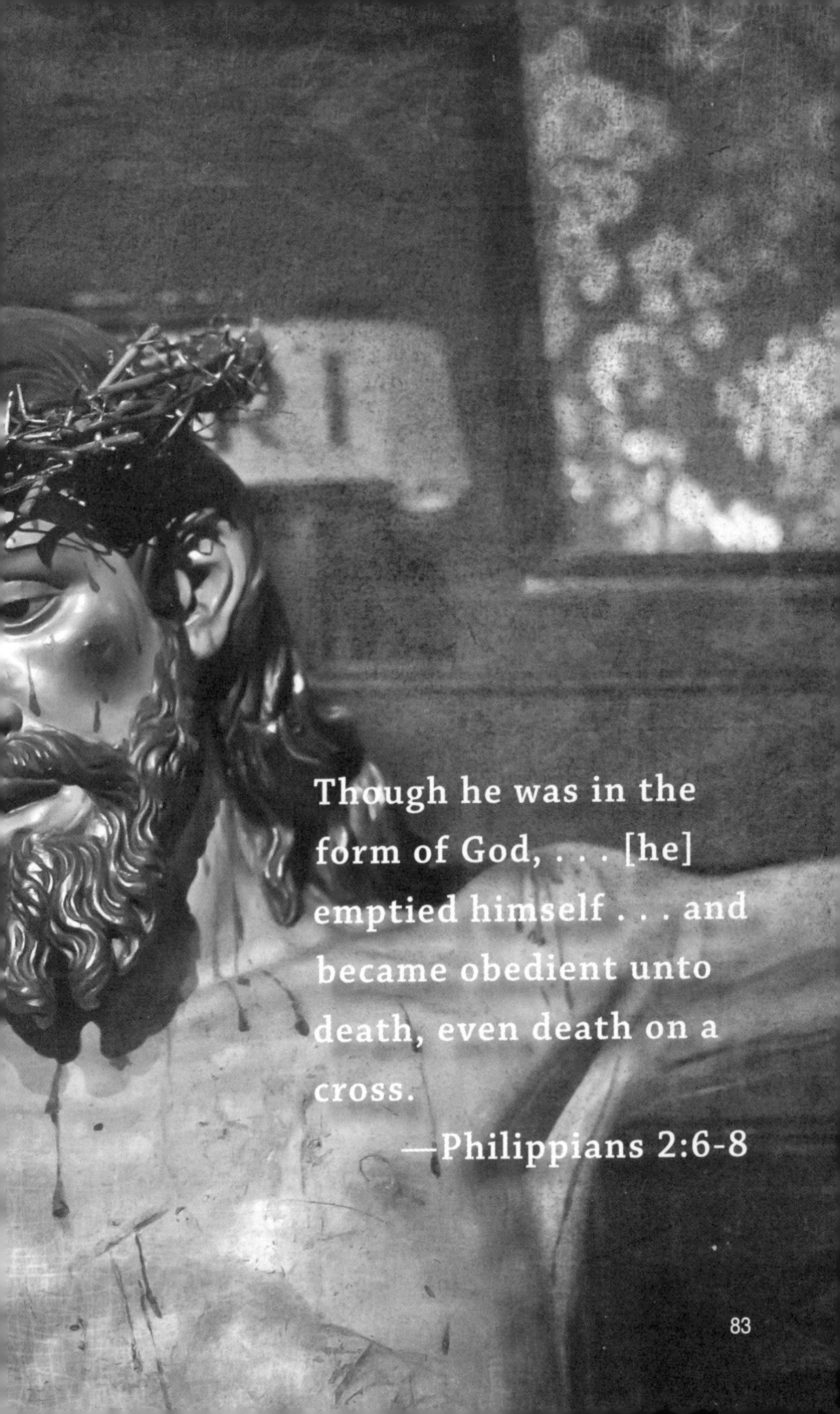

Though he was in the form of God, . . . [he] emptied himself . . . and became obedient unto death, even death on a cross.

—Philippians 2:6-8

Ask one person to lead the group in the following prayer to the Holy Spirit.[1] Or someone could pray in their own words, asking the Lord that through the reading of the passion story, Christ's suffering on the cross would become more real to every person in the group.

In the name of the Father, and of the Son, and of the Holy Spirit.

Leader | Let us take a moment of silence and call to mind God's presence here with us. **(Pause.)** Father, open our hearts and minds as we gather together in the name of your Son, Jesus. Believing in your presence and power, we pray together:

All Come, O Holy Spirit:
Enlighten my understanding to know your commands;
strengthen my heart
against the wiles of the enemy;
inflame my will . . .
I have heard your voice,
and I don't want to harden
my heart by resisting,
By saying "later . . . tomorrow."
Nunc coepi! Now!
Lest there be no tomorrow for me!
O, Spirit of truth and wisdom,
Spirit of understanding and counsel,
Spirit of joy and peace!
I want what you want,
I want it because you want it,
I want it as you want it,
I want it when you want it.
Amen.

—St. Josemaría Escrivá (1902–1975)[2]

[1] This prayer includes a Latin phrase, *nunc coepi*, meaning "Begin now!" *Nunc* is pronounced with a Spanish or Italian "u" ("noonck"). The American pronunciation of the Latin word *coepi* is "chay pee." But don't worry about the exact pronunciation. What matters is that the group is praying, "Holy Spirit, have your way. Begin your work in me now!"

[2] Accessed at http://stjosemaria.org/prayer-to-the-holy-spirit/.

Imagine that you have discovered that a close friend plans to betray you. How would this knowledge affect your interaction with that friend? What do you think Jesus felt and thought as he celebrated the Passover with his disciples, knowing that Judas had already made an agreement to betray him?

Ask someone to read the following Scripture passage aloud.

Matthew 26:14-29

14Then one of the twelve, who was called Judas Iscar-
iot, went to the chief priests 15and said, "What will
you give me if I deliver him to you?" And they paid
him thirty pieces of silver. 16And from that moment
he sought an opportunity to betray him.
17Now on the first day of Unleavened Bread the
disciples came to Jesus, saying, "Where will you have

us prepare for you to eat the passover?" [18]He said, "Go into the
city to such a one, and say to him, 'The Teacher says, My time is
at hand; I will keep the passover at your house with my disciples.'"
[19]And the disciples did as Jesus had directed them, and they prepared the passover.

[20]When it was evening, he sat at table with the twelve disciples;
[21]and as they were eating, he said, "Truly, I say to you, one of you
will betray me." [22]And they were very sorrowful, and began to say
to him one after another, "Is it I, Lord?" [23]He answered, "He who
has dipped his hand in the dish with me, will betray me. [24]The Son
of man goes as it is written of him, but woe to that man by whom
the Son of man is betrayed! It would have been better for that man
if he had not been born." [25]Judas, who betrayed him, said, "Is it I,
Master?" He said to him, "You have said so."

[26]Now as they were eating, Jesus took bread, and blessed, and
broke it, and gave it to the disciples and said, "Take, eat; this is my
body." [27]And he took a cup, and when he had given thanks he gave
it to them, saying, "Drink of it, all of you; [28]for this is my blood of
the covenant, which is poured out for many for the forgiveness of
sins. [29]I tell you I shall not drink again of this fruit of the vine until
that day when I drink it new with you in my Father's kingdom."

1. What struck you from this Gospel reading?

2. What strikes you about Jesus in this passage?

3. Catholic biblical scholar Fr. Daniel Harrington has observed that in Matthew's account of Jesus' last Passover, Jesus shows himself to be in control, willingly meeting his passion.[1] Would you agree with this observation? Why or why not?

4. What do you notice about Judas in this passage?

5. Contrast Jesus and Judas. What differences stand out to you?

6. What can you learn from Jesus' treatment of Judas, his betrayer?

7. What do you think this meal and conversation meant to the disciples at the time? What might it have meant to them after Jesus' death and resurrection?

8. We know that Jesus was tempted in every way that we are, yet was without sin (Hebrews 4:15). What were some of the human struggles and temptations Jesus could have suffered?

[1] Daniel J. Harrington, SJ, *Sacra Pagina* (Collegeville, MN: Liturgical Press, 1991), p. 369.

9. How does reflecting on Jesus' human struggles and temptations affect your relationship with him?

10. From this passage come the words we hear during every Mass: "Take, eat; this is my body" and "Drink of it, all of you." How does this passage or your discussion of it enrich your experience of receiving Christ in the Eucharist?

11. This week we accompany Jesus on his final steps to the cross. What are some practical ways we could be more focused and intentional so that we can more deeply encounter Jesus during Holy Week?

Group *Lectio Divina*

What follows are the first and second readings for Passion Sunday. The ancient practice of *lectio divina,* literally "divine reading," can help us enter into Scripture, allowing us to hear more profoundly what God wants to speak into our lives.

A gift to the whole Church from St. Benedict and the monastic tradition, *lectio divina* is an attentive listening to the voice of God through the books of sacred Scripture. It's a way of opening yourself to God through the Spirit-inspired word of God (cf. 2 Timothy 3:16). Scripture is *the* privileged text for encountering the living God.[2]

By reading a Scripture passage aloud slowly and prayerfully, the Spirit has the opportunity to speak particularly to each of us

[2] Vatican II, *Dei Verbum,* http://www.vatican.va/archive/hist_councils/ii_vatican_council/documents/vat-ii_const_19651118_dei-verbum_en.html.

through a word or phrase by making it stand out to us in some way. It might raise a question in your mind, grab your attention because you've never noticed it before, comfort you, or even disturb you. God communicates with each of us in the way that we can best hear him. All you need to do at first is to notice what catches your attention.

Repeated readings may deepen your focus on that word or phrase; at other times it may illuminate another word that completes what God wanted to speak to you that day. Sometimes a new message emerges altogether.

This prayerful reading of Scripture has inspired countless saints throughout the ages. It is a simple and accessible way to enter more fully into the Easter mystery. (To pray *lectio divina* at home, see Appendix B for a simple formula to help you remember the "Four Rs"—Read, Reflect, Respond, and Rest.)

The facilitator will read each passage aloud slowly, to allow some time for the group to reflect silently on the passage and/or ask a brief question. Group members should listen for what stands out each time it is read.

Isaiah 50:4-7

4The Lord GOD has given me
  the tongue of those who are taught,
that I may know how to sustain with a word
  him that is weary.
Morning by morning he wakens,
  he wakens my ear
  to hear as those who are taught.

5 The Lord GOD has opened my ear,
and I was not rebellious,
I turned not backward.
6 I gave my back to the smiters,
and my cheeks to those who pulled out the beard;
I hid not my face
from shame and spitting.

7 For the Lord GOD helps me;
therefore I have not been confounded;
therefore I have set my face like a flint,
and I know that I shall not be put to shame.

Philippians 2:5-11

5 Have this mind among yourselves, which was in Christ Jesus,
6 who, though he was in the form of God, did not count equality
with God a thing to be grasped, 7 but emptied himself, taking the
form of a servant, being born in the likeness of men. 8 And being
found in human form he humbled himself and became obedient unto death, even death on a cross. 9 Therefore God has highly
exalted him and bestowed on him the name which is above every
name, 10 that at the name of Jesus every knee should bow, in heaven
and on earth and under the earth, 11 and every tongue confess that
Jesus Christ is Lord, to the glory of God the Father.

Holy Week provides an opportunity for deeper conversion as we contemplate the passion, death, and resurrection of Christ. We can encounter the Lord in prayer, Scripture, and the sacramental life of the Church. That's why you should meet as a group to discuss the readings for Easter during the Octave of Easter, the eight days following Easter Sunday. This will allow you to spend extra time this week praying, reading Scripture, and participating in the liturgies of the Triduum.

If you have not had a chance to celebrate the Sacrament of Reconciliation this Lent, find a time to go this week. Even if you already have gone, consider going again. The Church encourages us to frequent this "sacrament of conversion," because in it Christ heals and continually transforms our inner life. Most parishes offer extra times for Confession during Holy Week to make the sacrament easily available.

If your small group would like to meet during Holy Week, you could watch the film *Jesus of Nazareth* by Franco Zeffirelli (1977). This widely acclaimed movie on the life of Christ brings the gospel story to life. Since small groups will not meet again until the week after Easter, you could gather on two or three evenings during Holy Week to view this six-hour film, or on a single evening to watch only the last two hours. Watching the conclusion on Good Friday is ideal. The movie can be found on various streaming services and in local libraries. Another option would be to watch the more recent film, *The Passion of the Christ* (2004), although many find the violence depicted in the scenes of Jesus' scourging and crucifixion difficult to watch.

Pray the Rosary this week using the sorrowful mysteries. If you aren't sure how to pray the Rosary, many resources are available online that can show you step-by-step how to do it.

Experience the summit of the liturgical year by participating in all three Triduum services. The Triduum begins with the celebration of the Mass of the Lord's Supper on Holy Thursday, during which Jesus' washing of the disciples' feet is reenacted and the Tabernacle is emptied. Good Friday is the only day of the year when Mass is not celebrated, but the liturgy includes the reverencing of the cross and many beautiful prayers, as well as the reading of the passion. Finally, you can celebrate Easter on Sunday or at the Vigil on Saturday evening, during which salvation history is recounted through multiple Scripture readings and catechumens are baptized.

Use the Scripture passages below or the daily Mass readings for prayer and reflection this week.

Scriptures Passages for Meditation:

- John 12:1-11
- Hebrews 4:14-16, 5:7-9
- Isaiah 52:13-53:12
- John 13:21-33, 36-38
- Isaiah 42:1-7
- John 18:1–19:42

This Week's Mass Readings:

Monday: Is 42:1-7 • Ps 27:1-3, 13-14 • Jn 12:1-11

Tuesday: Is 49:1-6 • Ps 71:1-6, 15, 17 • Jn 13:21-33, 36-38

Wednesday: Is 50:4-9 • Ps 69:8-10, 21-22, 31, 33-34 • Mt 26:14-25

Holy Thursday: Ex 12:1-8,11-14 • Ps 116:12-13, 15-18 • 1 Cor 11:23-26 • Jn 13:1-15

Good Friday: Is 52:13–53:12 • Ps 31:2,6,12-13, 15-17, 25 • Heb 4:14-16; 5:7-9 • Jn 18:1–19:42

Begin by offering prayers that arise from your discussion. When the group is ready to close, one of the participants can pray the penitential hymn *Attende Domine*, based on a tenth-century prayer for the Lenten season. All should pray the response together.

In the name of the Father, and of the Son, and of the Holy Spirit.

***Attende Domine* (Draw Near, O Lord)**

All Draw near, O Lord, our God; graciously hear us, guilty of sinning before you.

Leader O King exalted,
Savior of all nations,
See how our grieving lifts our eyes
to heaven;
Hear us, Redeemer, as we beg forgiveness.

All Draw near, O Lord our God; graciously hear us, guilty of sinning before you.

Leader Might of the Father, keystone of God's temple,
Way of salvation, gate to heaven's glory.
Sin has enslaved me;
Free your sons and daughters from bondage.

All Draw near, O Lord our God; graciously hear us,
guilty of sinning before you.

Leader We pray you, O God, throned in strength and splendor,
Hear from your kingdom, this our song of sorrow;
Show us your mercy;
Pardon our offenses.

All Draw near, O Lord our God; graciously hear us,
guilty of sinning before you.

Leader Humbly confessing countless sins committed,
Our hearts are broken, laying bare their secrets;
Cleanse us, Redeemer,
Boundless in compassion.

All Draw near, O Lord our God; graciously hear us,
guilty of sinning before you.

Amen.

Easter Sunday:
The Resurrection
of the Lord

Go to Galilee

“There they will see me.”
—Matthew 28:10

Unlike the previous sessions, when small groups met to discuss the upcoming week's readings, groups should meet to discuss the Easter readings *after* they are read at Mass on Easter Sunday. Meet sometime during the Octave of Easter (the eight days following Easter, including Divine Mercy Sunday). This allows participants to focus on the Triduum during Holy Week and also share their experiences of Holy Week during the final small group session.

Ask someone to pray in their own words, and then read aloud the following prayer slowly as others pray along silently.

In the name of the Father, and of the Son, and of the Holy Spirit.

O Death, where is thy sting?
O Hell, where is thy victory?
Christ is risen, and thou art overthrown!
Christ is risen, and the demons are fallen!
Christ is risen, and the angels rejoice!
Christ is risen, and life reigns!
Christ is risen, and not one dead remains in the grave!
For Christ, being risen from the dead,
has become the first fruits of those who have
fallen asleep.
To Him be glory and dominion unto ages of ages.

—Paschal Homily of St. John Chrysostom
(c. 349–407)

Amen.

Ask one person to read the narrator's part (N), another to read the angel's part (A), and a third person to read the words of Jesus (J).

Matthew 28:1-10

N: 1 Now after the sabbath, toward the dawn of the first day of the week, Mary Magdalene and the other Mary went to see the sepulchre. 2 And behold, there was a great earthquake; for an angel of the Lord descended from heaven and came and rolled back the stone, and sat upon it. 3 His appearance was like lightning, and his raiment white as snow. 4 And for fear of him the guards trembled and became like dead men. 5 But the angel said to the women,

A: "Do not be afraid; for I know that you seek Jesus who was crucified. 6 He is not here; for he has risen, as he said. Come, see the place where he lay. 7 Then go quickly and tell his disciples that he has risen from the dead, and behold, he is going before you to Galilee; there you will see him. Lo, I have told you."

N: 8 So they departed quickly from the tomb with fear and great joy, and ran to tell his disciples. 9 And behold, Jesus met them and said, "Hail!" And they came up and took hold of his feet and worshiped him. 10 Then Jesus said to them,

J: "Do not be afraid; go and tell my brethren to go to Galilee, and there they will see me."

1. What strikes you from this passage?

2. Place yourself in the shoes of Mary Magdalene in this scene. She sees the tomb of Jesus; the earth quakes and a glowing angel descends, rolls back the stone, and sits upon it. How did the guards react? How might you have reacted if you were Mary?

3. How does the angel minister to the women?

4. What emotions seize the two women as they run from the scene to share their experience with the disciples? What emotions arise in your heart when you think of sharing your experience of Jesus with others?

5. What happens as the women respond to the angel's directions? What can we learn from their response?

6. Verse 9 describes the women embracing Jesus' feet and worshiping him, giving him homage. What is "homage"? In what ways do you give homage to Jesus? Share any fruit that you have experienced from this.

7. Why do you think Jesus wants to meet his disciples in Galilee? (You may look ahead to the description of this meeting in Matthew 28:16-20.)

8. The apostle Paul wrote to the Corinthian church: "But if there is no resurrection of the dead, then Christ has not been raised; if Christ has not been raised, then our preaching is in vain and your faith is in vain" (1 Corinthians 15:13-14). Why is the resurrection so central to the Christian faith? How does the resurrection influence your daily life as a Christian?

9. How, in the last six weeks of Lent, have you experienced within yourself the paschal mystery, the death and resurrection of Jesus Christ? Has anything in you died, or has something new come to life?

10. Although our path as Christians includes the way of the cross, how might we live out that way with joy and hope, as a resurrection people? What has helped you to live your faith more joyfully and hopefully?

If you have time, you could read and discuss the excerpt on pages 104–106 from Pope Francis' 2014 Easter Homily in "Connection to the Cross This Week."

Read and reflect on this excerpt from Pope Francis:

After the death of the Master, the disciples had scattered; their faith had been utterly shaken, everything seemed over, all their certainties had crumbled and their hopes had died. But now that message of the women, incredible as it was, came to them like a ray of light in the darkness. The news spread: Jesus is risen as he said. And then there was his command to go to *Galilee*; the women had heard it twice, first from the angel and then from Jesus himself: "Let them go to Galilee; there they will see me." . . .

Galilee is *the place where they were first called, where everything began!* To return there, to return to the place where they were originally called. Jesus had walked along the shores of the lake as the fishermen were casting their nets. He had called them, and they left everything and followed him (cf. Matthew 4:18-22).

To return to Galilee means *to reread* everything on the basis of the cross and its victory, . . . to reread everything—Jesus' preaching, his miracles, the new community, the excitement and the defections, even the betrayal—to reread everything starting from the end, which is a new beginning, *from this supreme act of love.*

For each of us, too, there is a "Galilee" at the origin of our journey with Jesus. "To go to Galilee" means something beautiful; it means rediscovering our baptism as a living fountainhead, drawing new energy from the sources of our faith and our Christian experience. To return to Galilee means above all to return to that blazing light with which God's grace touched me at the start of the journey. From that flame I can light a fire for today and every day, and bring heat and light to my brothers and sisters. That flame ignites a humble joy, a joy which sorrow and distress cannot dismay, a good, gentle joy.

In the life of every Christian, after baptism there is also . . . *a more existential "Galilee"*: the experience of *a personal encounter with Jesus Chris*t who called me to follow him and to share in his mission. In this sense, returning to Galilee means treasuring in my heart the living memory of that call, when Jesus passed my way, gazed at me with mercy, and asked me to follow him. To return there means reviving the memory of that moment when his eyes met mine, the moment when he made me realize that he loved me.

The Gospel is very clear: we need to go back there, to see Jesus risen, and to become witnesses of his resurrection. This is not to go back in time; it is not a kind of nostalgia. It is returning to our first love, in order to *receive the fire* which Jesus has kindled in the world and to bring that fire to all people, to the very ends of the earth.

—Pope Francis, Easter Vigil Homily, April 19, 2014[1]

[1] Accessed at https://w2.vatican.va/content/francesco/en/homilies/2014/documents/papa-francesco_20140419_omelia-veglia-pasquale.html.

Here are some questions to consider if you are reading this as a group:

1. Did anything stand out to you from Pope Francis' homily? Reflect for a moment on why God might have drawn that to your attention. **(Pause.)** Would someone be willing to share what struck you and why?

2. Do you feel you have your own "Galilee," a period of time, or a "moment when he made me realize that he loved me"? How did you experience this?

3. Would someone be willing to share about a time when things looked dark in your life, but the power of the resurrection came to you, "like a ray of light in the darkness"?

Whether or not you read and discussed the questions above in a group, spend some time on your own reflecting on those instances when you experienced the power of the resurrection in a dark time. Recall them with "grateful remembrance" (Pope Francis, *Evangelii Gaudium,* 13). What does this experience mean to you today? How does it affect the way you live?

Lenten observances forge a deeper connection with the cross of Jesus' passion, but Easter reminds us to celebrate by living in the spirit of Jesus' resurrection. It is so easy to celebrate at the pinnacle of Easter Sunday but quickly forget that we're living in

Christ's victory *every* day! To help us live the resurrection joyfully and fully, the Church has made Easter an entire season, fifty days leading us all the way to the coming of the Holy Spirit at Pentecost.

Take time this week to establish spiritual practices for the Easter season that can ground you in the power and joy of the resurrection. Death has been defeated! Claim Jesus' victory for yourself—he did it for you! You will find suggestions for how to do that in the final section of this book, "Connection to the Cross for Life."

Use the Scripture passages below or the daily Mass readings for prayer and reflection this week.

Scripture Passages for Meditation:

- Acts 2:42-47
- John 20:19-23
- Acts 6:1-7
- John 10:1-10
- Acts 8:1-8
- John 17

This Week's Mass Readings:

Monday: Acts 2:14, 22-33 • Ps 16:1-2, 5, 7-11 • Mt 28:8-15
Tuesday: Acts 2:36-41 • Ps 33:4-5, 18-20, 22 • Jn 20:11-18
Wednesday: Acts 3:1-10 • Ps 105:1-4, 6-9 • Lk 24:13-35
Thursday: Acts 3:11-26 • Ps 8:2, 5-9 • Lk 24:35-48
Friday: Acts 4:1-12 • Ps 118:1-2, 4, 22-27 • Jn 21:1-14
Saturday: Acts 4:13-21 • Ps 118:1, 14-21 • Mk 16:9-15

The group could begin extemporaneously: thanking Jesus for his sacrifice on the cross, praising the Father for raising Jesus from the dead, thanking the Holy Spirit for how he has moved hearts during Lent, and asking blessings for each person in the group. Close the shared prayer by saying together the following prayer by Blessed John Henry Newman.

In the name of the Father, and of the Son, and of the Holy Spirit.

Dear Jesus,
Help us to spread your fragrance
everywhere we go.
Flood our souls with your spirit and life.
Penetrate and possess our whole being
so utterly
that all of our lives may be only a radiance
of yours.
Shine through us.
And be so in us, that every soul we come in
contact with
may feel your presence in our soul.
Let them look up and see no longer us but
only Jesus!

Stay with us, and then we shall begin to shine as
you shine;
so to shine as to be a light to others.
The light, O Jesus, will be all from you;
none of it will be ours; it will be you,
shining on others through us.
Let us thus praise you in the way you love best
by shining on those around us.
Let us preach you without preaching,
not by words but by our example, by the
catching force,
the sympathetic influence of what we do,
the evident fullness of the love our hearts bear to you.
Amen

—Adapted from a prayer by
Blessed John Henry Newman (1801–1890)[1]

[1] Accessed at http://totus2us.com/vocation/blesseds/bl-john-henry-newman/.

“It is no longer because of your words that we believe, for we have heard for ourselves, and we know that this is indeed the Savior of the world.” (John 4:42)

Let’s return to where we began—the word of God spoken to us through the prophet Joel: “Return to me with all your heart” (2:12). We pray that your Lenten journey has been a movement of the heart, drawing you closer to Christ. This is what traditional Lenten penitential practices are meant to do: lead you to greater interior conversion and *metanoia*—a change of heart and mind, which is the meaning of repentance—so that you can live in the power of Jesus’ resurrection.

This guide afforded a time for small groups to gather together as Christians to be strengthened for the journey, much as the first-century disciples did: “And they devoted themselves to the apostles’ teaching and fellowship, to the breaking of bread and the prayers” (Acts 2:42). The apostles’ teaching included the stories of Jesus’ life that were eventually written down in the Gospels. The earliest disciples discussed the meaning of what the Lord had said and done, just as your group has done.

Your group may want to continue meeting during the Easter season or resume meeting again in the fall. The Evangelical Catholic offers many small group discussion guides, which are found on our website, evangelicalcatholic.org. Or you could read a book of the Bible together. Some favorite epistles for small groups include Philippians, Ephesians, and 2 Corinthians. Working through a whole Gospel will greatly increase your experience of Jesus and your knowledge about the years of his ministry. If you meet during the Easter season, you might want to read the Book of Acts, which describes the joy and fruitfulness that characterized the early Church.

For your own Easter reflection, revisit any notes you made in this book in the "Connection to the Cross" sections. Those insights are meant to be lived in the victory that Christ has won for us. As St. Paul enthusiastically told us, "We are *more* than conquerors through him who loved us" (Romans 8:37, emphasis added). As you review, seek to find again the gifts that the Holy Spirit offered during each session. By identifying with Jesus' temptations in the desert, have you been emboldened to face your own temptations? By acknowledging spiritual blindness, can you receive the light of God's grace in a new way when darkness enfolds you? By experiencing Jesus on a deeply personal level, as did the Samaritan woman at the well, will you overflow with the living water of God to everyone you encounter?

Commit to continuing the prayer practices during the Easter season that most inspired you in the weekly "Connection to the Cross" exercises. Try to attend daily Mass at least once or twice a week or even daily; it will help you receive God's peace. Build on the practice of meditating on Scripture so that the Lord can speak a personal word to you within it. Don't neglect the Sacrament of Reconciliation, a guaranteed opportunity for life-transforming grace; it holds the promise of a different future. The world-changing, death-destroying, expansive potential of the early Church continues in us. We can realize the power of the resurrection and the presence of the Holy Spirit, in our own lives and in the world, when we encounter Christ in prayer and the sacraments.

Easter is all about new life. If Lent is a time to be moved interiorly in our hearts, then Easter is a time to move exteriorly, into action. The Holy Spirit will inspire us to want to love and serve the world in a way that perfectly fits the gifts we have to offer. It's as if God has made us for a particular ministry or service—because he did!

Christ is risen! You are a "new creation" (2 Corinthians 5:17), the living body of Christ on earth, called to redeem and renew all that God has made. The resurrection of Jesus assures us that his victory lives on in us, his followers. We can move forward in complete confidence, heeding the call he puts on our hearts. Jesus, our faithful Shepherd, is by our side.

Pray the following prayer through the Easter season to keep the power of the resurrection fresh in your heart and mind:

> Ever living God, help me to celebrate with joy the power of your resurrection and to express in my life the love I have known in Christ Jesus.
>
> Incarnate Word among us, speak to me with clarity, that I might know your perfect will and walk in the grace of your revelation.
>
> Eternal Spirit, breathe new life into me and animate my gifts, that I may set the world ablaze and advance the reign of God in my family and every family, my neighborhood and every neighborhood, my nation and every nation.
>
> In the power of the resurrection, let me press on in victory, O Holy One, and proclaim the gospel to all peoples, to the glory of God the Father. Amen.

Appendices for Participants

Ⓐ Small Group Discussion Guidelines

Ⓑ A Guide to Seeking God in Prayer and Scripture

Ⓒ A Guide to the Sacrament of Reconciliation

Appendix A

A small group seeks to foster an honest exploration of Jesus Christ with one another. For many, this will be a new experience. You may be wondering what will take place. Will I fit in? Will I even want to come back?

Here are some expectations and values to help participants understand how small groups work, as well as what makes them work well and what doesn't. When a group meets for the first time, the facilitator may want to read the following aloud and discuss it to be sure everyone understand small group parameters.

Purpose

We gather as searchers. Our express purpose for being here is to explore together what it means to live the gospel of Jesus Christ in and through the Church.

Priority

In order to reap the full fruit of this personal and communal journey, each one of us will make participation in the weekly gatherings a priority.

Participation

We will strive to create an environment in which all are encouraged to share at their comfort level.

We will begin and end all sessions in prayer, exploring different ways to pray together over time. We will discuss a Scripture passage at every meeting. Participants do not need to read the passage beforehand—no one needs to know anything about the Bible in order to participate. The point is to discuss the text and see how it applies to our own lives.

Discussion Guidelines

The purpose of our gathering time is to share in "Spirit-filled" discussion. This type of dialogue occurs when the presence of the Holy Spirit is welcomed and encouraged by the nature and tenor of the discussion. To help this happen, we will observe the following guidelines:

- Participants strive always to be respectful, humble, open, and honest in listening and sharing: they don't interrupt, respond abruptly, condemn what another says, or even judge in their hearts.

- Participants share at the level that is comfortable for them personally.

- Silence is a vital part of the experience. Participants are given time to reflect before discussion begins. Keep in mind that a period of comfortable silence often occurs between individuals speaking.

- Participants are enthusiastically encouraged to share while at the same time exercising care to permit others (especially the quieter members) an opportunity to speak. Each participant should aim to maintain a balance: participating without dominating the conversation.

- Participants keep confidential anything personal that may be shared in the group.

- Perhaps most important, participants should cultivate attentiveness to the Holy Spirit's desire to be present in the time spent together. When the conversation seems to need help, ask for the Holy Spirit's intercession silently in your heart. When someone is speaking of something painful or difficult, pray that the Holy Spirit comforts that person. Pray for the Spirit to aid the group to respond sensitively and lovingly. If someone isn't participating, praying for that person during silence may be more helpful than a direct question. These are but a few examples of the ways in which each person might personally invoke the Holy Spirit.

Time

We will meet weekly because that is the best way to become comfortable together, but we can schedule around any breaks or holidays when many people will be away. We can discuss options for continuing to meet after we have completed all the sessions.

It is important that our group start and end on time. Generally a group meets for about ninety minutes, with an additional thirty minutes or so afterwards for refreshments. Agree on these times as a group, and work to honor them.

The 1% Challenge: Spending Time with God in Prayer and Scripture

Unless you are convinced that prayer is the best use of your time,you will never find time to pray.
—Fr. Hilary Ottensmeyer, OSB[1]

If I only I had the time!

Time—we only have so much of it each day. All kinds of demands chip away the hours. Modern communication and social media increase our sense of urgency. No wonder we experience conflicting desires over how to spend our time.

Most of us struggle to make room for what we know, deep down, is most important in life: nurturing our relationships, helping and caring for others, and pursuing positive goals and dreams. But when it's difficult to find time for even our family and dear friends, a relationship with God can become a very low priority.

One thing we all know for certain: time is an essential ingredient in any meaningful, life-giving relationship. Friendships don't form or last unless people spend time together. Marriages struggle when spouses don't find time to "be there" for one another: to talk and listen deeply. Parents who do not or cannot prioritize time with their children know the pain this can cause down the road.

[1] Accessed at http://www.saintmeinrad.edu/seminary-blog/echoes-from-the-bell-tower/posts/2015/monastic-time/.

Trust, friendship, communication, and love—they all require time. Some things never change. We were made for relationships, and relationships require time: slow, intentional, focused, attentive quality and quantity time.

So how about our relationship with God?

We believe that God is with us always (Matthew 28:20). Our relationship with God, as a father's or mother's with a child, doesn't depend only on our effort or our deliberate attempts to build that relationship. Yet a deepening friendship with God, like all relationships, depends on time spent together. What kind of relationship do you have with the person in the neighborhood with whom you've never had personal time, although you take in her garbage can weekly because she is disabled? She is an acquaintance, not a friend. Friends spend time together. Jesus called us his friends (John 15:15). Friendship requires focused attention on other people and real loving engagement in the interactions you have with them.

We spend time with our friend Jesus at Mass. The Mass remains the center, source, and summit of our prayer lives. But without more time with Jesus, that encounter at Mass can resemble seeing that neighbor at a block party: celebrating and talking for a few minutes, without any deep connection. The mysterious reality of that person remains remote.

Time is often the missing piece that makes friendship with God possible. Time changes everything: our experience of Mass, our experience of one another, and our relationship with God—the only One who heals and changes our lives.

How much time should I spend in quiet prayer?

A little goes a long way with God. We give an inch; God gives a mile. That's how much he wants a relationship with you. Do you want a relationship with him? *Take the 1% Challenge: spend at least fifteen minutes each day alone with God.*

One percent of twenty-four hours is just fourteen minutes and twenty-four seconds of your day. Round that up to fifteen minutes. All of us can find fifteen minutes in our day if we truly desire God in our lives. Commit yourself to that 1%, and we promise that you will

- begin to know the Lord on a more personal level;
- grow in your ability to hear God's voice and heed his wise guidance for you;
- experience more of the Lord's love, peace, and joy—even through difficult circumstances;
- become more virtuous and attentive to other people, because in prayer, Christ gives us his own compassion for each person.

It is not easy, at least not at first. But prayer begets prayer. As you experience the fruit of a relationship, your desire for God grows. Your heart seeks more and more to *build your life around prayer* rather than just trying to squeeze it into your day. Hunger for God grows when you taste the sweetness of Jesus' company and experience the joy of a Christ-centered life.

How should I spend my fifteen minutes?

Always begin by recognizing that God is with you. He is with you even when you're not paying attention. When you focus on him, you are simply focusing on reality.

St. Teresa of Avila called prayer "an intimate sharing between friends." Any good friendship involves three things: talking, listening, and simply being together.

1. Talk to God

There is no wrong way to talk to God. Talk about anything on your mind. Keep it real; don't just say what you think a prayerful person should say. Even saying, "Lord, help me to pray" is itself a prayer.

Keep in mind the first three things we all learn to say as children: *"Thank you," "I'm sorry,"* and *"Please."* That's a great outline for a chat with God—it's as simple as that!

2. Listen to God

"Morning after morning he opens my ear that I may hear" (cf. Isaiah 50:4).

No matter how impossible it may seem, we were made to hear and heed the good and loving counsel of the Lord. "My sheep hear my voice, and I know them, and they follow me," says Jesus (John 10:27). This is attainable!

The fastest way to improve your ability to recognize the voice of God is to read the Scriptures prayerfully. The Bible truly is God's word expressed in human words. With the Holy Spirit coming to our aid, reading it becomes "a life-giving encounter," as St. John Paul II wrote (*Novo Millennio Ineunte*, 39). On the following pages, we've included a simple outline of *lectio divina*, a time-tested way of encountering the voice of the living God in Scripture.

3. Be with God

The only way to hear anyone, including God, is to be silent. Any friendship in which you are never quiet and attentive will eventually dissolve. The Lord says, "Be still, and know that I am God" (Psalm 46:10).

Begin and end each prayer time with a minute of silence to rest in God's presence. Imagine the beloved disciple, John, who at the Last Supper rested his head against Jesus' chest. What a beautiful image for us: to lean on him and simply rest. If you notice that your mind is wandering, remind yourself again that you are with God. Then rest again, leaning on Jesus' chest. If you find that image helpful, go back to it when you are again distracted. Distraction happens, but Jesus remains! If it's not helpful, find your own way to recenter on Jesus. God will guide you if you ask!

Sometimes words get in the way of deeper communication. Lovers stare into one another's eyes wordlessly. Parents and children cuddle and say nothing.

St. John of the Cross said, "Silence is God's first language." You may not hear anything audible or even sense any interior communications, but be confident that God is filling that silence in ways you cannot immediately perceive. Often something can become very clear later in the day after a time of silence in the morning.

Lectio Divina: Prayerful Reading of Scripture

"Speak, Lord, your servant is listening." (cf. 1 Samuel 3:10)

Remember that God is with you—really.

Quiet yourself and invite the Holy Spirit to guide your prayer time. Take a minute or so just to breathe deeply and focus your attention on God. Perhaps repeat a simple phrase like "Come, Holy Spirit," or repeat the name of Jesus with each breath.

1. Read the Scripture selection. Digest it slowly in small sections. If a word, phrase, or verse stands out, pay attention! That might be the Holy Spirit communicating to you.

2. Reflect on the meaning of whatever most stands out to you. Ponder that word or phrase. If nothing stands out, try summarizing the passage: recount what happened in your own words. It may help to go back to the text and notice what you may have missed; sometimes a word or phrase will strike you on a second or third reading. Another way to aid your reflection, if nothing stands out, is to imagine yourself in the scene. Notice any questions that arise or any emotions you experience. This is often the way God draws your attention to a topic. You might also see promises to claim, commands to obey, examples to follow, errors to avoid, sins to repent of, or praises to sing. You may wish to write these down.

3. Respond & Resolve. Talk to God as you would speak to a parent, sibling, or trusted friend. If the Holy Spirit leads you to any resolution or application in your life, write it down to help you remember. Ask God to help you to live it out. Ask Mary or another saint to intercede for you.

4. Rest in God's presence for a few minutes of silence.

Recommended Scripture Passages for *Lectio Divina*

Choose passages that are relatively short. The goal is not to cover a lot of material but to listen "with the ear of our heart," as St. Benedict instructed his monks in his Rule.

- Read the Gospel passage of the day for the Mass, which can be found online at http://www.usccb.org/nab.
- Slowly work through a Gospel or an epistle, such as Philippians, James, or 1 John.
- Read the psalms.
- Search online for inspirational passages that pertain to various moods and situations in your life. For example, you can search "the Bible on anxiety" or on any other topic, such as hope, fear, trust, or forgiveness.
- Search online for various reading plans that take you through the Bible in a set number of days.
- Pray with an app. There are many available that will guide you through prayer and that can fit into your 1% time slot. One, called "Pray as You Go," leads you through a contemplative time in God's word.

Tips

- Spend this time exclusively with God, not while driving or doing other activities.

- To allow time for conversation and silence with God, avoid devotions during your fifteen minutes (such as the Rosary or the Divine Mercy Chaplet). By all means, pray devotions; they are a rich gift of the Church. But let the 1% be a different mode of interaction with God. If you spoke only poetry to your spouse, your marriage would be in trouble!

- A scheduled time helps build the habit of prayer. Setting a regular time each day for prayer is vital. Ideally, it should be first thing in the morning. This is the easiest way to make sure that your fifteen minutes of prayer happen. Nothing can interfere with your prayer time if you pray before everything else begins. But the important thing is to pray—however and whenever you can. It's more important to schedule a realistic time each day than to schedule an ideal time that you won't keep or to try to pray at the same time each day if your daily schedule varies widely.

- If fifteen minutes is too difficult at first, start with a more achievable goal and work up to 1%.

- If you're already faithful to 1%, consider working up to 2%! Perhaps you can offer the additional time for others or for some special intention.

- If you miss a day, don't get discouraged; just get back on track. Try especially hard not to miss two days in a row.

- Notice the fruit (the results in your life) on days that you pray. That will motivate you to pray every day.

- Keep a notebook with brief insights, prayers, and Scripture passages that speak to you.

- Try the 1% Challenge for thirty days at first and evaluate your experience. Even if it takes you forty days to do thirty days of 1% prayer, don't be hard on yourself. Celebrate when you complete thirty days!

- To keep yourself accountable and to really grow, find a spiritual companion—a friend who also has committed to the 1% Challenge. Get together monthly or every two weeks to discuss your experiences, goals, and growth. "As iron sharpens iron, so one person sharpens another" (cf. Proverbs 27:17).

We only devote periods of quiet time to the things or the people whom we love; and here we are speaking of the God whom we love, a God who wishes to speak to us.

—Pope Francis (*The Joy of the Gospel*, 146)

My secret is simple. I pray.

—St. Teresa of Calcutta

Appendix C

If it has been a long time since you last went to Confession—or if you've never been—you may be hesitant and unsure. Don't let these very common feelings get in your way. Reconciling with God and the Church always brings great joy. Take the plunge—you will be glad you did!

If it will help to alleviate your fears, familiarize yourself with the step-by-step description of the following process. Most priests are happy to help anyone willing to take the risk. If you forget anything, the priest will remind you. So don't worry about committing every step and word to memory. Remember, Jesus isn't giving you a test; he just wants you to experience the grace of his mercy!

Catholics believe that the priest acts *in persona Christi,* "in the person of Christ." The beauty of the sacraments is that they touch us both physically and spiritually. On the physical level in Confession, we hear the words of absolution through the person of the priest. On the spiritual level, we know that it is Christ assuring us that he has truly forgiven us. We are made clean!

You usually have the option of going to Confession anonymously—in a confessional booth or in a room with a screen—or face-to-face with the priest. Whatever your preference will be fine with the priest.

Steps in the Sacrament of Reconciliation:

1. Prepare to receive the sacrament by praying and examining your conscience. If you need help, you can find many different lists of questions online that will help you examine your conscience.

2. Once you're with the priest, begin by making the Sign of the Cross while greeting the priest with these words: "Bless me, Father, for I have sinned." Then tell him how long it has been since your last confession. If it's your first confession, tell him so.

3. Confess your sins to the priest. If you are unsure about anything, ask him to help you. Place your trust in God, who is a merciful and loving Father.

4. When you are finished, indicate this by saying, "I am sorry for these and all of my sins." Don't worry later if you have forgotten something. This closing statement covers everything that didn't come to mind in the moment. Trust God that he has brought to mind what he wants you to address.

5. The priest will assign you a penance, such as a prayer, a Scripture reading, or a work of mercy, service, or sacrifice.

6. Express sorrow for your sins by saying an Act of Contrition. Many versions of this prayer can be found online. If memorization is difficult for you, just say you're sorry in your own words.

7. The priest, acting in the person of Christ, will absolve you of your sins with prayerful words, ending with "I absolve you from your sins in the name of the Father, and of the Son, and of the Holy Spirit." You respond by making the Sign of the Cross and saying, "Amen."

8. The priest will offer some proclamation of praise, such as "Give thanks to the LORD, for he is good" (Psalm 136:1). You can respond, "His mercy endures forever."

9. The priest will dismiss you.

10. Be sure to complete your assigned penance immediately or as soon as possible.

Appendices for Facilitators

Appendix D

Perhaps no skill is more important to the success of a small group than the ability to facilitate a discussion lovingly. It is God's Holy Spirit working through our personal spiritual journey, not necessarily our theological knowledge, that makes this possible.

The following guidelines can help facilitators avoid some of the common pitfalls of small group discussion. The goal is to open the door for the Spirit to take the lead and guide your every response because you are attuned to his movements.

Pray daily and before your small group meeting. This is the only way you can learn to sense the Spirit's gentle promptings when they come!

You are a Facilitator, Not a Teacher

As a facilitator, it can be extremely tempting to answer every question. You may have excellent answers and be excited about sharing them with your brothers and sisters in Christ. However, a more Socratic method, by which you attempt to draw answers from participants, is much more fruitful for everyone else and for you as well.

Get in the habit of reflecting participants' questions or comments to the whole group before offering your own input. It is not necessary for you as a facilitator to enter immediately into the discussion or to offer a magisterial answer. When others have sufficiently addressed an issue, try to exercise restraint in your comments. Simply affirm what has been said; then thank them and move on.

If you don't know the answer to a question, have a participant look it up in the *Catechism of the Catholic Church* and read it aloud to the group. If you cannot find an answer, ask someone to research the question for the next session. Never feel embarrassed to say, "I don't know." Simply acknowledge the quality of the question and offer to follow up with that person after you have done some digging. Remember, you are a facilitator, not a teacher.

Affirm and Encourage

We are more likely to repeat a behavior when it is openly encouraged. If you want more active participation and sharing, give positive affirmation to the responses of the group members. This is especially important if people are sharing from their hearts. A simple "Thank you for sharing that" can go a long way in encouraging further discussion in your small group.

If someone has offered a theologically questionable response, don't be nervous or combative. Wait until others have offered their input. It is very likely that someone will proffer a more helpful response, which you can affirm by saying something such as "That is the Christian perspective on that topic. Thank you."

If no acceptable response is given and you know the answer, exercise great care and respect in your comments so as not to appear smug or self-righteous. You might begin with something such as "Those are all interesting perspectives. What the Church has said about this is . . . "

Avoid Unhelpful Tangents

Nothing can derail a Spirit-filled discussion more quickly than digressing on unnecessary tangents. Try to keep the session on track. If conversation strays from the topic, ask yourself, "Is this a

Spirit-guided tangent?" Ask the Holy Spirit too! If not, bring the group back by asking a question that steers conversation to the Scripture passage or to a question you have been discussing. You may even suggest kindly, "Have we gotten a little off topic?" Most participants will respond positively and get back on track through your sensitive leading.

That being said, some tangents may be worth pursuing if you sense a movement of the Spirit. It may be exactly where God wants to steer the discussion. You will find that taking risks can yield some beautiful results.

Don't Fear the Silence

Be okay with silence. Most people need a moment or two to come up with a response to a question. People naturally require some time to formulate their thoughts and put them into words. Some may need a few moments just to gather the courage to speak at all.

Regardless of the reason, don't be afraid of a brief moment of silence after asking a question. Let everyone in the group know early on that silence is an integral part of normal small group discussion. They needn't be anxious or uncomfortable when it happens. God works in silence!

This applies to times of prayer as well. If no one shares or prays after a sufficient amount of time, just move on gracefully.

The Power of Hospitality

A little hospitality can go far in creating community. Everyone likes to feel cared for. This is especially true in a small group whose purpose it is to connect to Jesus Christ, a model for care, support, and compassion.

Make a point to greet people personally when they first arrive. Ask them how their day has been going. Take some time to invest in the lives of your small group participants. Pay particular attention to newcomers. Work at remembering each person's name. Help everyone feel comfortable and at home. Allow your small group to be an environment where authentic relationships take shape and blossom.

Encourage Participation

Help everyone to get involved, especially those who are naturally less vocal or outgoing. To encourage participation initially, always invite various group members to read aloud the selected readings. Down the road, even after the majority of the group feels comfortable sharing, you may still have some quieter members who rarely volunteer a response to a question but would be happy to read.

Meteorology?

Keep an eye on the "Holy Spirit barometer." Is the discussion pleasing to the Holy Spirit? Is this conversation leading participants to a deeper personal connection to Jesus Christ? The intellectual aspects of our faith are certainly important to discuss, but conversation can sometimes degenerate into an unedifying showcase of intellect and ego. Other times discussion becomes an opportunity for gossip, detraction, complaining, or even slander. When this happens, you can almost feel the Holy Spirit leaving the room!

If you are aware that this dynamic has taken over a discussion, take a moment to pray quietly in your heart. Ask the Holy Spirit to help you lead the conversation to a more wholesome topic. This can often be achieved simply by moving to the next question.

Pace

Generally, you want to pace the session to finish in the allotted time, but sometimes this may be impossible without sacrificing quality discussion. If you reach the end of your meeting and find that you have covered only half the material, don't fret! This is often the result of lively Spirit-filled discussion and meaningful theological reflection.

In such a case, you may take time at another meeting to cover the remainder of the material. If you only have a small portion left, you can ask participants to pray through these on their own and come to the following meeting with any questions or insights they might have. Even if you must skip a section to end on time, make sure you leave adequate time for prayer and to review the "Connection to the Cross This Week" section. This is vital in helping participants integrate their discoveries from the group into their daily lives.

Genuine Friendships

The best way to show Jesus' love for and interest in your small group members is to meet with them for coffee, dessert, or a meal outside of your small group time.

You can begin by suggesting that the whole group get together for ice cream or some other social event at a different time than when your small group usually meets. Socializing will allow relationships to develop. It provides the opportunity for different kinds of conversations than small group sessions allow. You will notice an immediate difference in the quality of community in your small group at the next meeting.

After that first group social, try to meet one-on-one with each person in your small group. This allows for more in-depth conversation and personal sharing, giving you the chance to know each participant better so that you can love and care for them as Jesus would.

Jesus called the twelve apostles in order that they could "be with him" (Mark 3:14). When people spend time together, eat together, laugh together, cry together, and talk about what matters to them, intense Christian community develops. That is the kind of community Jesus was trying to create, and that must be the kind of community we try to create, because it changes lives. And changed lives change the world!

Joy

Remember that seeking the face of the Lord brings joy! Nothing is more fulfilling, more illuminating, and more beautiful than fostering a deep and enduring relationship with Jesus Christ. Embrace your participants and the entire spiritual journey with a spirit of joyful anticipation of what God wants to accomplish.

"These things I have spoken to you, that my joy may be in you, and that your joy may be full." (John 15:11)

Appendix E

The following notes will help you be better prepared to facilitate each session. They include suggestions for helping participants become comfortable with the group, for dealing with sensitive topics and difficult questions, for learning to pray aloud together, and for celebrating the resurrection together. Review the notes for each session as you prepare each week.

1st Sunday of Lent: Step into the Desert

Extemporaneous prayer requires that we talk to God as if he is really there and really listening—because he is! During a recited prayer, it's easy for the person who isn't the reader to lose focus. The prayer, even if it is beautiful and inspiring, could fail to address the genuine concerns of those in the group.

That's why in Week 1, we encourage the group, if at all possible, to pray extemporaneously. You should come prepared to demonstrate this way of praying at the first session. Hearing you pray spontaneously gives the members of your group a model of praying aloud in their own words, which may be completely new to them. The written opening prayers in every session should be used after a period of extemporaneous prayer; only as a last resort should they be used by themselves. The closing prayers can be used in conjunction with extemporaneous prayer that speaks to what has happened during the session. It's far better to pray a sputtering sentence or two that comes from the heart than to meticulously read a beautiful but potentially less relevant written prayer. This applies for every session.

Jesus' forty days in the desert, an intense time of fasting and confronting the very real presence of evil, is the primary model for Lent. During this season, the Holy Spirit leads us, too, into a "desert place," if we're willing to follow his lead. In the desert, we can experience the desolation of sin and realize once again our absolute dependence on God.

The opening discussion and the short reflection from Henri Nouwen will help the group think together about preparing for Lent. Our objective during Week 1 is to help participants to consider deeply during their private prayer how Lent could sow seeds of transformation in their hearts.

Inherent in this Gospel and in all the Lenten readings is the idea that hardships and desert experiences, like those of Jesus, are not always just wretched times to be endured, but can also be opportunities for God to draw us closer and minister to us. "In everything God works for good with those who love him" (Romans 8:28). God can use desert deprivation and temptation to bring forth riches from some of the most barren periods of our lives.

For a beautiful personal application of the temptations of Jesus, read Henri Nouwen's *In the Name of Jesus.*[1]

[1] Henri Nouwen, *In the Name of Jesus: Reflections on Christian Leadership* (New York: Crossroads Publishing, 1992).

2nd Sunday of Lent: Strength for the Journey

For the sake of time, please invite only one or two members of the group to share experiences for the opening discussion.

You may wish to review Exodus 34:29-35, the Old Testament prefiguring of the transfiguration. This is not essential but will add some depth to the story of Mount Tabor that could enrich your preparation. The second reading, 2 Timothy 1:8-10, touches on the difficult problem of the role of faith and works in our salvation, an issue that has often divided Catholics and Protestants. Lest there be any confusion, the Catholic Church teaches that we are saved by grace through faith in Jesus Christ. Only God's gratuitous offer makes eternal life possible; we don't earn it (see *Catechism of the Catholic Church,* 1996–2005).

This teaching could raise questions about the value of our actions, including sacrificial Lenten penitential practices. If this happens, first ask the group if anyone has a response to the concern. Should an adequate answer fail to surface, explain that the Church presents a classic "both/and" scenario concerning this question. While it is true that salvation comes only through the gracious gift of God, it is also true that God asks us to cooperate with that grace so that it can bear fruit in our lives and in the world. It is as if God has given us a gift, but we have to open it.

Even our ability to cooperate with God's saving initiative in our lives is an extension of divine grace. Paul expresses this beautifully in his letter to the Ephesians: "For by grace you have been saved through faith; and this is not your own doing, it is the gift of God—not because of works, lest any man should boast. For we are his workmanship, created in Christ Jesus for good works, which God prepared beforehand, that we should walk in them" (2:8-10). Works aren't the cause of our salvation; they result from it.

If a satisfactory conclusion doesn't emerge, ask the person most interested in this to do some research and report back at the next meeting.

3rd Sunday of Lent: Experience Living Water

Giving some background information about Jewish attitudes toward Samaritans will help provide context for this session. In response to Question 2, if participants aren't aware of how remarkable Jesus' interaction with the Samaritan woman is, offer a brief teaching. Jews and Samaritans had a long and antagonistic relationship stemming from multiple causes. The Samaritans, following a different strand of Hebrew practice, refused to worship in Jerusalem. Jews looked down on them for intermarrying with Assyrians (Gentiles), who had invaded them.[1] In addition, because Samaria was situated in between Jerusalem and Galilee, Jews had to pass through unfriendly and sometimes dangerous territory as they traveled

[1] Raymond E. Brown, SS, *The Gospel According to John I–XII* (Garden City, NY: Double Day, 1966), p. 170.

back and forth for religious festivals observed by a pilgrimage to the Temple.[2]

Because of these religious, cultural, and political divisions, Jews simply didn't speak to Samaritans, particularly male Jews to female Samaritans. It is extraordinary that Jesus would even approach this woman in a public place, and even more astonishing that he asked her for a drink of water. Samaritan women were considered ritually impure. Jews were forbidden to accept any water from them in their unclean vessels. The Samaritan woman asks how Jesus expects to get water when he doesn't even have his own bucket because normally a Jew would never use *her* bucket! The way that Jesus breaks down all barriers to reach out to this woman should encourage the group members to trust that Jesus will show the same mercy and persistence in reaching out to them.

4th Sunday of Lent: Live in the Light

The opening discussion question about experiences of the Sacrament of Reconciliation could elicit short, clipped answers or divert into lengthy tales of painful experiences with priests, or uneasiness with the whole idea of telling one's sins to another person. Don't allow tales of negative Confession experiences to take up too much time. If someone describes a positive

[2] Raymond E. Brown, SS; Joseph A. Fitzmyer, SJ, and Roland E. Murphy, OCarm, *New Jerome Biblical Commentary* (Englewood Cliffs, NJ: Prentice Hall, 1990), p. 701.

experience, focus on that. Asking questions to draw out more details on why and how the sacrament gave the person life and hope in a specific situation will help shift attention away from sometimes entertaining but not always edifying stories.

Don't ignore participants who share negative experiences or personal opinions on the value of the sacrament. Respond judiciously, recognizing that such Confession experiences may well have been painful, frightening, or mortifying for that person. If someone expresses the opinion that Confession is not valuable, recognize what he or she says, and then turn to drawing out others' positive experience or sharing your own. Listen compassionately while trying to protect the group from hearing about too many negative stories or opinions.

Question 3 about the progression of the blind man's responses reveals his increasing spiritual insight. Question 4 regarding the Pharisees' responses displays the parallelism John employed in constructing this passage (but if you need to eliminate a question because of time constraints, skip this one). While on the one hand, the man born blind is growing in insight and ends up professing faith in Jesus, the Pharisees' interrogations reveal the opposite—their hardening blindness.

In reviewing "Connection to the Cross This Week," encourage participants to take time to examine their consciences in preparation for Reconciliation that week. An examination of conscience guide can be found online at http://www.usccb.org/prayer-and-worship/sacraments-and-sacramentals/penance/examinations-of-conscience.cfm.

5th Sunday of Lent: A Matter of Life and Death

The Lazarus story is very rich. Your conversation could go in any number of directions that are worth pursuing. Pray and seek the leading of the Holy Spirit on how far to pursue any theme that emerges.

As always, if someone doesn't know or can't explain why a passage stands out to them, ask that person some questions and involve the other group members to elicit discussion. Sometimes hearing someone else's comments about the Scripture passage can become a word from the Holy Spirit for that person, helping them to understand why God drew their attention to these words. If the discussion touches on the topics addressed in upcoming questions, skip or modify these to avoid repetition.

Question 7 asks the group to speculate about Jesus' motivation. Assure your group that there is no wrong answer. When we try to imagine or speculate why Jesus did something, we give the Holy Spirit an opening, allowing him to prompt our thoughts and considerations.

Palm Sunday: The Passion of the Lord

This session is intended for the week prior to Palm Sunday. If your group began meeting after Lent had already started, the session can take place during Holy Week. (A reminder: we suggest that small groups schedule the Easter session during the Octave of Easter, the week following the Triduum.) This session for Palm Sunday also includes an alternative suggestion for groups that want to meet during Holy Week: watching a movie of the passion as a group. This is entirely optional.

In order to jump into the session, save the spontaneous prayers for the closing prayer and take a brief and simple approach to the opening prayer. As you prepare, be sure to leave at least ten minutes for the closing prayer. It is easy to consistently shorten the time spent in prayer at the end in order to allow more time for discussion. Leaving ten minutes for the closing prayer allows time for each person to internalize more deeply the reflection and discussion you have shared.

With such a sobering reading about Judas' betrayal of Jesus, a more meditative and prayerful closing seems fitting as group members prepare for Palm Sunday and the Lord's passion. That is why we include the communal *lectio divina* in this session. The instructions appear below. Because these instructions are designed for a group, they differ from the directions for personal *lectio divina* in Appendix B.

Read through these several days in advance of the reading. For this to be a prayerful experience for the group, you need to be familiar with what you're going to say and do. If you want to ask someone else to read aloud, do that in advance of the meeting so that the person can practice and become familiar with the Scripture passages.

1. Begin by offering a prayer on behalf of the group, inviting the Holy Spirit to open each person's heart to God's word and to the messages that God has for each person.

2. Either read aloud the passage yourself, or invite a participant who will be able to read slowly and well. Encourage group members to be attentive to any word or phrase that strikes them; whether it raises a question, bothers them, consoles them, or challenges them doesn't matter. God works in many ways!

3. Allow a minute or two of silent reflection: participants quietly consider the word or phrase that God has drawn to their attention in the Scripture passage.

4. Invite all participants to share only the word or phrase without elaboration. You could share first, or ask someone else to begin.

5. Either read aloud the passage again yourself, or invite the reader to do so. The group should again be attentive to any other word or phrase that strikes them.

6. Allow another minute or two of silent reflection. Then invite the group to quietly consider what the Lord might be speaking into their lives from this Scripture passage. Allow another minute of silence.

7. Invite all participants to share the following: "I hear the Lord saying to me . . . " Ask participants to restrict their comments to what they hear the Lord saying, not how God may be calling them into action.

8. Invite a third participant to read the same passage once more. Ask the group to allow God to elaborate on the words or phrases that stood out to them.

9. Allow a minute of two of silent reflection. Ask the group to silently consider, “What does the Lord want me to do today or this week?” Allow another minute of silence.

10. Invite any participant who is willing to share the following: “I believe the Lord wants me to . . . ”

11. Allow time for silent prayer. If the Spirit leads you, you could invite the group to pray for those who have voiced actions the Lord wants them to take. A simple formula should make this easy: “Lord, we pray that ____________ will have the courage and the determination necessary to (describe action).” Then elaborate with requests specific to that person and what the Lord wants them to do.

12. Conclude by praying together the Lord’s Prayer or moving directly to the closing prayer, reviewing “Connection to the Cross this Week” afterward.

Easter Sunday: Go to Galilee

Easter is the pinnacle of the Christian life, as the readings demonstrate, and the celebration of the Easter liturgy is the climax of Lent. It would be a sad thing to meet for all of Lent but never celebrate Easter together! Make sure you meet during the

Octave of Easter while the mystery and beauty of Jesus' resurrection are still fresh in your mind.

Seek to facilitate a conversation that recognizes the joy and hope of the resurrection. The resurrection should be a great comfort and inspiration to followers of Jesus. If God can redeem even the crucifixion, that torturous, ignominious death, then God can redeem our own pain and suffering and that of the whole world. We will "walk through the valley of the shadow of death" (Psalm 23:4), but the Good Shepherd, Jesus, risen from the dead, will be with us. We may die with Jesus thousands of ways in this lifetime, but we will rise with him in glory.

For the discussion of the Scripture passage, you may want to make copies of Matthew 28:16-20, referenced in question 7, unless your group regularly brings their Bibles with them. For that question, about the importance and implications of the resurrection, the goal is for answers to emerge from the group discussion. If that doesn't happen despite your best efforts to facilitate conversation, you may refer to the following list of the consequences of the resurrection. However, under no circumstances should you read these! Try to find ways that you can put these concepts into your own words, or better yet, develop questions to help your group explore them.

- Through the resurrection, God definitively demonstrated Jesus' divine identity as his Son (Romans 1:4).

- Because of the resurrection, we have been born again into a "living hope" (1 Peter 1:3), not only that we will also be resurrected on the last day, but that we can live out our days on earth in the power of the resurrection.

- The resurrection made it possible for the God of Abraham, Isaac, and Jacob to be the God of Jew and Gentile alike (Acts 26:22-23).

- The resurrection completes the mystery of our salvation. By his death on a cross, Jesus freed us from sin; by his resurrection, Jesus restored us to new life in him.

Appendix F

Opening Prayer

We have provided a guided opening prayer for each session because it can help people who are completely new to small groups and shared extemporaneous prayer feel more at ease. If everyone or most people present are already comfortable speaking to God aloud in their own words in a group, you won't need these prayers at all. It's always better to talk to God from our hearts in a small group. It contributes to the intimacy of the group and also builds individual intimacy with God.

Since some people have never witnessed spontaneous prayer, it's part of your role to model it. Prayers from the heart spoken aloud demonstrate how to talk to God honestly and openly. Seeing someone pray this way expands a person's understanding of who God is and the relationship they can have with Jesus Christ.

You can grow in extemporaneous prayer by praying aloud directly to Jesus during your personal prayer time and as you prepare for the group. This will help "prime the pump," so to speak.

Even if you enjoy praying aloud spontaneously, your goal as a facilitator is to provide opportunities for everyone to grow spiritually. People who pray aloud with others grow in leaps and bounds—we've seen it! After the first meeting, tell the group that you will allow time at the end of your extemporaneous prayer for others to voice prayers. As soon as the group appears to have grown into this, invite other people to open the group with prayer instead of leading it yourself or using the prayer provided.

If you don't do it in the first meeting, in the second week, pray the opening prayer in your own words. Here are some simple parts to include:

1. Praise God! Say what a great and wonderful God our Father is. Borrow language from the psalms of praise if you don't have your own. Just search online for "praise psalms."

2. Thank God! Thank the Lord for the gift of gathering together. Thank him for giving each person present the desire to sacrifice his or her time to attend the group. Thank him for the blessing of your parish or campus community.

3. Ask God for your needs. Ask God to bless your time together and to make it fruitful for all present as well as for his kingdom. Ask Jesus to be with you, who are two or three gathered in his name. Ask the Holy Spirit to open hearts, illuminate minds, and deepen each person's experience of Lent through the Scripture passages you'll read and discuss. Ask the Holy Spirit to guide the discussion so that you can all grow from it.

4. Close by invoking Jesus: "We pray this through Christ our Lord" or "We pray this in Jesus' name."

5. End with the Sign of the Cross.

Some Essentials for Extemporaneous Prayer:

- Speak in the first-person plural "we." For example, "Holy Spirit, we ask you to open our hearts . . . " It's fine to add a line asking the Holy Spirit to help you facilitate the discussion as he wills, or something else to that effect, but most of the prayer should be for the whole group.

- Model speaking directly to Jesus our Lord. This may sound obvious, but among Catholic laypeople, it isn't frequently practiced or modeled. This is a very evangelical thing to do in the sense that it witnesses to the gospel. Not only does it show how much we believe that the Lord loves us, but it also demonstrates our confidence that Jesus himself is listening to us! As we say our Lord's name, we remind ourselves, as well as those who hear us, that we aren't just talking to ourselves. This builds up faith.

You and anyone unaccustomed to hearing someone pray to Jesus directly may feel a bit uncomfortable at first. But group members will quickly become more at ease as they hear these prayers repeatedly and experience more intimacy with Jesus. Bear in mind always that many graces come from praying "the name which is above every name" (Philippians 2:9).

If you've never publicly prayed to Jesus, you may feel childish at first, but pray for the humility of a child. After all, Jesus did say that we need to become like children (Matthew 18:3)! The more we pray directly to Jesus in our personal prayer, the less awkward it will feel when we pray to him publicly.

- Model great faith and trust that the Lord hears your prayer and will answer it. It's terrific just to say in prayer, "Jesus, we trust you!"

- You can always close extemporaneous prayer by inviting the whole group to join in a prayer of the Church, such as the Glory Be, the Our Father, or the Hail Mary. This will bring all into the prayer if previously, just one person was praying aloud extemporaneously.

Closing Prayer

For the closing prayer, we recommend that you always include extemporaneous prayer, even if you also use the prayer provided. No written prayer can address the thoughts, concerns, feelings, and inspirations that come up during the discussion.

If some group members already feel comfortable praying aloud in their own words, invite the group to join in the closing prayer right away. If not, wait a week or two. Once you feel that the group has the familiarity to prevent this from being too awkward, invite them to participate. You could tell the group that you will begin the closing prayer, and then allow for a time of silence so that they can also pray aloud. Make sure they know that you will close the group's prayer by leading them into an Our Father after everyone is done praying spontaneously. This structure helps people feel that the time is contained and not completely lacking in structure. That helps free them to pray aloud.

On the next page are some possible ways to introduce your group to oral extemporaneous prayer. Don't read these suggestions verbatim—put them into your own words. It's not conducive to helping people become comfortable praying aloud spontaneously if you are reading out of a book!

"The closing prayer is a great time to take the reflections we've shared, bring them to God, and ask him to help us make any inspirations a reality in our lives. God doesn't care about how well-spoken or articulate we are when we pray, so we shouldn't either! We don't judge each other's prayers. Let's just pray from our hearts, knowing that God hears and cares about what we say, not how perfectly we say it. When we pray something aloud, we know that the Holy Spirit is mightily at work within us because it's the Spirit who gives us the courage to speak."

"Tonight for the closing prayer, let's first each voice our needs to one another; then we will take turns putting our right hand on the shoulder of the person to the right of us and praying for that person. After we each express our prayer needs, I will start by praying for Karen on my right. That means that I need to listen carefully when she tells us what she needs prayer for. We may not remember everyone's needs, so be sure to listen well to the person on your right. I'll voice my prayer needs first; then we'll go around the circle to the right. Then I will begin with the Sign of the Cross and pray for ___________ (name of person to the right) with my hand on her/his shoulder. Okay? Does anyone have any questions?"

Connection to the Cross This Week

These weekly prayer and reflection exercises allow Jesus to enter more fully into the hearts of you and your small group members. If we don't give God the time that allows him to work in us, we experience far less fruit from our small group discussions. Prayer and reflection water the seeds that have been planted during the small group so that they can take root. Without the "water" of prayer and reflection, the sun will scorch the seed, and it will shrivel up and die, "since it had no root" (Mark 4:6). Encountering

Christ during the week on our own makes it possible for us to be "rooted in Christ" (cf. Colossians 2:7) and to drink deeply of the "living water" (John 4:10) that he longs to pour into our souls.

Please review the "Connection to the Cross This Week" section in advance so that you're familiar with it, and then review it together as a group during each meeting. Reviewing it together will show everyone that it is an important part of the small group. Ask for feedback each week about how these prayer and reflection exercises are going. Don't spend too long on this topic, however, especially in the early weeks while members are still becoming comfortable together and growing more accustomed to praying on their own. Asking about their experience with the recommended prayer, sacrament, or spiritual exercise will help you know who is hungry for spiritual growth and who might need more encouragement. The witness of participants' stories from their times of prayer can ignite the interest of others who are less motivated to pray.

About The Evangelical Catholic

The Evangelical Catholic (EC) equips Catholic ministries for evangelization by inspiring, training, and supporting local leaders to launch dynamic outreach. Through training events, services, and ongoing contractual relationships, the EC forms and trains Catholic pastoral staff and lay leaders for long-term evangelical efforts that can be locally sustained without ongoing site visits and regular consulting.

To accomplish this mission, we equip the lay faithful to invite the lost into the joy of life in Christ and stem the tide of Catholics leaving the Church. We form pastoral staff to make disciples, shepherd evangelistic ministries, and manage pastoral structure to make discipleship to Jesus the natural outcome within the parish or university campus ministry.

Our prayer is that through the grace of the Holy Spirit, we can help make the Church's mission of evangelization accessible, natural, and fruitful for every Catholic, and that many lives will be healed and transformed by knowing Jesus within the Church.